Christopher W. Nolan

MANAGING
the
Reference
Collection

AMERICAN LIBRARY ASSOCIATION
Chicago and London
1999

While extensive effort has gone into ensuring the reliability of information appearing in this book, the publisher makes no warranty, express or implied, on the accuracy or reliability of the information, and does not assume and hereby disclaims any liability to any person for any loss or damage caused by errors or omissions in this publication.

Project editor: Joan A. Grygel

Cover, text design, and composition: Douglas & Gayle

Printed on 50-pound White Offset a pH-neutral stock, and bound in 10-point coated cover stock by McNaughton & Gunn

The paper used in this publication meets the minimum requirements of American National Standard for Information Sciences—Permanence of Paper for Printed Library Materials, ANSI Z39.48-1992. ∞

Library of Congress Cataloging-in-Publication Data
Nolan, Christopher W.
    Managing the reference collection / Christopher W. Nolan.
        p.   cm.
    Includes bibliographical references (p.   ) and index.
    ISBN 0-8389-0748-2 (acid-free paper)
    1. Libraries—United States—Special collections—Reference books.
    I. Title.
    Z711.N65   1998
    025.5′2′068—dc21   98-37178

Printed in the United States of America.

03 02 01 00 99   5 4 3 2 1

❧ Contents ❧

◌◊ Preface ◊◌

Earlier, when I wrote an article on the principles of selection and weeding for the reference collection, I was convinced that reference collection management received too little attention from librarians. This impression was apparently shared by a number of colleagues because I received many positive responses for my coverage of that subject. Several other works were written on reference collection management during the early 1990s, showing that a similar concern was emerging. In the nearly eight years since that time, we have all witnessed an amazing transformation of our reference services by the burgeoning number of databases available on CD-ROM and online, as well as the arrival of the Internet as both a reference tool with useful content and a competitor for our users' attention. It is likely that we are seeing a major change in some of the ways that we will provide reference materials to our library users. On the other hand, the evaluation and selection that we have traditionally performed with the world of printed resources seem just as useful and necessary a task with the new electronic world. Systematic management of our reference collections should provide us with a method for dealing with this wide variety of resources in the current atmosphere of rapid change.

This book is a guide for those who are just beginning to think about managing reference collections and for those who have been doing this for some time. The aim is to provide reference selectors with a framework for their selection and management activities. In the current world of expanding electronic resources and libraries with shrinking purchasing power, it is more important than ever that librarians work toward the creation of a lean, efficient reference collection that is based on actual user needs. Thus the first chapter begins with a discussion of reference collection fundamentals, those principles that, when followed, lead to a more rationally and economically chosen collection. Following chapters explore facets of who should do the managing, what criteria can be used to make good choices, and how budgets can be stretched as far as possible. The first chapter is a bit theoretical, but the book is designed to be a practical guide for those making decisions about the reference collection. Most of the chapters can be read out of sequence, although the first chapter's conclusions are reflected in all of the other chapters.

This book is not meant to compete with the standard reference services textbooks, which provide excellent treatments of a wide variety of reference issues. Nor is it meant to serve as a guide to reference materials. Instead, it gives a fuller picture of the selection and maintenance activities that are only briefly treated in textbooks. Some overlap in subject matter exists in the criteria for selecting print and electronic sources, but I hope that the slant on these subjects is sufficiently helpful to create some discussion among practicing reference selectors. Although my background is in university and college libraries, I have attempted to consider these issues from the position of public and school libraries as well. These collection management concepts are equally applicable to the reference collection with 50,000 volumes or with 500.

ɞ Acknowledgments ɷ

I would like to thank Marlene Chamberlain at ALA Editions for suggesting that I write a monograph for them, and I appreciate her patience as a few deadlines became objects in our memories. Additionally, Joan Grygel greatly enhanced the clarity of my text with her copy editing.

Much of the research for this book was accomplished during an academic leave from my position as head of reference at Trinity University. I would like to thank both the university administration and my colleagues for the chance to have a few months to work on this without my normal duties.

I have been honored to work with an exceptionally talented group of librarians and staff at Trinity over the past eleven years. All have been committed to providing the best possible service to our students and faculty. Frequent discussions and even disagreements about the treatment of our reference sources with reference colleagues have provided me with many opportunities to reflect on this subject. I would particularly like to thank Craig Likness for his many good suggestions years ago on my reference selection article, a debt that I forgot to mention in that article. I wish to acknowledge the support and ideas of my cataloging colleagues, especially Beverley Geer and Beatrice Caraway, who have worked with me on reference serials and other cataloging problems for several years and have always kept our users' needs in mind. Reference collection maintenance is always easier when reference has a solid working relationship with cataloging and acquisitions personnel. Much of the maintenance itself has been ably performed by Meredith Elsik for the last eight years, and I appreciate her awareness of and communication about the types of problems described in this volume. Having relied on professional library materials often held by other libraries, I must also acknowledge the helpfulness and efficiency of our interlibrary loan staff, Maria McWilliams and Herlinda Barrientos, who did their usual fine job of getting everything for which I asked, even cheerfully providing me with second copies of items I had misplaced.

In the same week that this manuscript was completed and shipped, I also celebrated the completion of another milestone: the first twenty years of my marriage to Lisa, a project that has taken much longer than the book, but one that has been infinitely easier. I am most appreciative of the patience and support that Lisa has shown during these months of research and writing, a time that has often taken me away from my usual family activities. She contributed several useful suggestions along the way. My sons, Jeremy and Patrick, have been helpful when I have needed quiet time or the use of the family computer at home. Their delight in reading books as well as their affinity for electronic sources strengthens my convictions that the coming years will require information and entertainment in a wide variety of media, including books and periodicals as well as computer-based sources. This book is gratefully dedicated to Lisa, Jeremy, and Patrick.

❧ 1 ❧

Reference Collection Fundamentals

The selection of sources for library reference collections and the decisions about how they should be maintained are tasks that a reference librarian often performs without much time for contemplation. The needs to stay abreast of new publications and to find the best sources on which to spend the acquisitions budget call for ongoing action. However, those who manage any part of the reference collection development process can profit from reflection on the reasons behind the creation and maintenance of this central collection.

The Importance of the Reference Collection

Why do we need a book on managing the reference collection? Reference librarians who use this collection on a daily basis will have no doubt about its centrality to their work, but literature on its development and management has only begun to become more common in our professional journals in the last fifteen years or so. Some may wonder if the collection is important enough to warrant separate treatment from the other collections in a library. Stop for a moment and consider these characteristics of reference collections:

Reference departments and their collections are usually located in very prominent locations in libraries so that users can easily find them. Mary and Victor Biggs have called this "highest-priority library space," places that should be occupied only by something of high usefulness to the library's community.[1]

Expenditures for reference materials make up a significant portion of most libraries' budgets. Indeed, many reference serials are among the most expensive serials purchases for libraries.

Reference librarians use the reference collection, along with the library's catalog, as the principal tool for aiding users who seek help. The quality of the answers that these users receive is based in no small part on the resources brought to bear on the problem.

Users ascribe considerable authority to this collection. They see reference librarians turn to the collection and pull out answers that seemed impossible for the users to find. The books do not circulate and thereby appear more valuable. Instruction librarians hand out lists of key reference titles during class sessions and also display such lists or guides in information stands.

Because many users start their information searches with indexes, encyclopedias, and bibliographies, what they find cited in the reference collection influences what materials they will retrieve from the remainder of the collection (or what items they will request via interlibrary loan). "The reference collection is a demand generator for the entire collection, its leading edge."[2]

With the growing numbers of full-text and numeric databases being made available in reference departments, these sources are frequently being used instead of the rest of the library's collections.

Finally, the reference resources available to users have an impact on how the users perceive the entire library. Users who expect to find certain titles or types of titles in the reference collection may think the library is generally deficient when the library does not own these titles.

Thus we see that librarians and users alike consider the reference collection quite important, and considerations about how to manage this highly used, expensive collection are warranted.

Some Thoughts about Terminology

There have been debates about the use of the terms "collection development" versus "collection management." "Collection development" has been the most-used term for quite a few years, and it no doubt reflects the overall trend of library collections to get larger in size over time. Also, discussions and implementations of weeding, or deselection of library materials, have been much less frequent than they have been for selecting and adding materials. Reasons for this vary, from the difficulty librarians have with discarding any materials to worries about censorship claims over withdrawn items to the political mandate to show the largest possible collection size for comparison with other libraries. Consequently, the literature of collection development has mostly emphasized growing collections.

Proponents of the phrase "collection management" correctly point out that merely adding new materials does not keep a collection in proper condition. Stacks become cluttered with deadwood, those outdated items that do not serve the library's clientele. Growth of the collection may be unbalanced, giving greater or lesser emphasis to parts of the collection that need adjustment to match user needs. The library may be running out of space to house the collection, and some items may need to be weeded. Furthermore, as is common today, library budgets may be losing buying power and, in areas such as serials, the net number of titles is shrinking, not growing.

Of course, many librarians who are well-versed in the necessary management issues still prefer to call their activity "collection development." Perhaps thinking about other uses of the word "development" could mute criticism of this term. "Career development," for example, refers to the enhancement of an employee's skills. Institutions that strive to develop their employees are not necessarily trying to add new workers; they are trying to "grow" the talents and potential contributions of the current workers. Likewise, collection development should be construed as the efforts of library staff to increasingly match the usefulness of their collection to the needs of the library users. Consequently, the two terms are used interchangeably in the following chapters. The phrase "collection development" is well entrenched in our literature and need not be avoided. Reference collection development, done well, requires attention to quality, not just quantity. In fact, good reference collection development may actually require a collection to decrease in size.

What Are Reference Sources?

Our reference collections consist of a variety of materials used to support reference functions. Though various formats are included, most of the items tend to be either printed books and serials or, increasingly these days, some form of electronic product. Most librarians appear to agree on which sources can be labeled reference sources and which cannot, regardless of whether the item should be purchased or should be shelved somewhere other than the reference collection. Is there something about these materials that intrinsically makes them useful for reference purposes? How do we define "reference source"?

One way is to revert to the traditional definitions given in various dictionaries. For example, this definition appears in *The ALA Glossary of Library and Information Science:*

> **reference book**   1. A book designed by the arrangement and
> treatment of its subject matter to be consulted for definite items
> of information rather than to be read consecutively. 2. A book
> whose use is restricted to the library building.[3]

This definition helps us somewhat by providing information about how these types of books are used and administered. The first definition is quite relative; different readers use books differently, so any item could be a reference book for a particular reader. (Some writers believe this makes any definition of a reference source based on its own internal characteristics impossible.)[4] For example, in Trinity University's library, students in a Biblical literature class write papers on the interpretation of a chosen set of verses. Most of the students will use commentaries—monographs written about one or more Biblical books—that will consider in turn each verse and chapter in these books. Commentaries are generally written as consecutive prose, and some readers will, in fact, read the books cover to cover. However, many of our students will quickly turn to the brief section that describes their chosen verses and ignore the rest. They are using the commentaries as reference books, though most libraries will shelve all but a few comprehensive commentaries in the circulating stacks.

Assertions that any book can be a reference book may be superficially true, but they do little to help us decide what should appropriately be shelved in our reference collections. Most libraries have reference collections, or at least items that are designated as reference sources, and the staff who give them the reference designation must follow some guidelines to make their choices. The *ALA Glossary* definition indicates that at least part of the difference resides in the usefulness of reference sources for consultation. Reference books are consulted by users who refer to them to retrieve definite items of information. Nonreference sources are more likely to be read consecutively. What makes consultation more effective with a reference book than with nonreference sources?

Marcia Bates argues that the key feature of a reference book is that it consists largely of files. Files are organized collections of records, the "information individuals." The records themselves are composed of one or more fields, the actual bits of data. These files are arranged in a particular order that facilitates retrieving a record from the files.[5] For example, a bibliography contains a principal file that arranges records for bibliographic sources into a particular order—say, by subject—and then may also provide additional files, such as indexes of the individual fields in those records (authors' names, titles, date of publication, and so on). An encyclopedia usually presents its records (in this case, articles) in alphabetical order, whether in the main file (the principal text entries) or in its index file; a historical outline may arrange its records in chronological order.

A reference book does not necessarily present information that cannot be found elsewhere in the library's collection. It instead represents the information and provides an arrangement and additional points of access to it. This repackaging and enhanced access increases the readers' ability to find the pieces of data more quickly than they could by browsing through texts of continuous exposition.

To verify her description of a reference book, Bates analyzed a sample of books from reference collections and from the circulating stacks at several libraries. She found that one could easily predict which of these two locations would be used for a book based on its percentage of files. Those books with a majority of the text set up as files and records were most likely to be shelved in reference, while those with a preponderance of continuous expository text were shelved in the stacks. Most books fell to one end of the spectrum or the other; that is, few titles consisted roughly of equal parts exposition and files.[6]

Classifying a book as a reference book based on what proportion of it is composed of information files correlates well with the typical decisions made in reference departments. My colleagues will consistently assign a book composed of a two hundred-page essay and a thirty-page bibliography to the circulating stacks. However, they would be much more likely to assign the book to the reference collection if it contained two hundred pages of bibliography and a thirty-page introductory essay. The first title is predominantly continuous exposition, and we do not expect a user to refer to this title for a quick consultation, although that is always possible. The second title, composed mainly of files and records, is not intended for cover-to-cover reading but was created for readers to consult and retrieve discrete units of information.

Thus, a better definition of "reference source" would be

> A *reference source* is a source designed for consultation rather than continuous reading, predominantly composed of ordered files arranged to facilitate rapid retrieval of pieces of information.

Certainly some titles are placed in reference collections that appear to be exceptions to this definition. Some are placed there for administrative reasons, such as preventing their theft. However, there is no reason why these need to go into reference; other library locations, such as reserves, could serve as well. Quite a few more titles that are frequently shelved in reference appear to be largely continuous text and therefore contrary to this definition: sacred books, law reporters, handbooks, and classic histories (for example, the *Cambridge History of China*). But Bates explains that these sources are "authoritative texts."[7] Although some of these sources may be read extensively in a continuous fashion, they are frequently used to answer a quick question or give a brief overview of a topic. Many of the texts have been marked up to include precise labels for their pieces of information; for example, the Bible has its book, chapter, and verse apparatus, and law reporters have their case citations and authoritative numeration of pages. Many reference queries can be solved by looking up a particular Biblical reference, a court decision, or a name or date from a large historical work. In the same way, an authoritative textbook can serve much like a subject encyclopedia. Any of the above sources can be considered reference sources if they provide the necessarily rapid retrieval of data, but if the reader must plow through pages of narrative text searching for verification of one fact, its reference usefulness should be suspect.

Electronic Sources

Do electronic sources fit into this definition? There is no reason to exclude the proliferating digital tools. The most common electronic sources in reference collections today include the library's online catalog, national bibliographic utilities, periodical indexes and abstracts, and encyclopedias. Libraries are also collecting increasing numbers of full-text and image databases. The former sources are composed largely of digital versions of sources that have previously existed in printed form. The electronic forms of indexes, encyclopedias, etc., are clearly performing the same types of reference functions as their print counterparts: providing rapid retrieval of citations, definitions, and facts.

However, the full-text and image databases bring up some different issues in terms of definitions. For example, one of the popular periodical databases, ProQuest's *Periodical Abstracts,* can be purchased as just a digital indexing and abstracting service, which offers faster and more-sophisticated retrieval using indexes for the various fields. It is also possible to subscribe to a version that contains the full text or page images of many of the articles that are indexed; therefore, users may search the full text of the articles, not just the traditional access points. Once a desired article is identified, the user can read the full article or print it out for later reading. Is the full-text version predominantly a reference source, designed for quick consultation, or is it a collection of articles from which some are selected and then read continuously? Obviously, this type of source serves both purposes. It would most likely be purchased for its reference functionality as a bibliographic index, yet a library's bibliographers would want to consider the implications of adding the electronic periodical titles that it includes. However, this is fundamentally a reference tool with the addition of the original text or images for some of its records.

The previous example describes an index that adds article text for some of its citations. A different example is a source that was originally created as a continuous text or image source but now provides searching features. For example, several scholarly journal publishers now allow access to their entire issues through an Internet subscription. Project Muse, for instance, provides online access to more than forty titles from Johns Hopkins University Press. While it is possible to do keyword searches across the journal files, just as one would do in a periodical index, this is basically a collection of journal issues online. How likely is it that users needing to search bibliographic indexes for a subject will intentionally choose to search a collection of just one publisher's journals? More likely, users will turn to this set of files when they are interested either in particular articles already identified from other sources or when they already know they are interested in searching one particular journal. Thus, while an electronic source of this type can be used for reference, its primary purpose would appear to be increasing the availability of and access to continuous text.

The nature of new electronic tools such as those just described is not totally clear, and we will likely see experimentation with their design in the near future. Most of this book's chapters will apply to electronic sources as well as print and other media, but some additional discussion of the issues involved in selecting and managing the new electronic tools is presented in chapter 5.

The Uses of the Reference Collection

Users of the reference collection include both the library's patrons and the reference department staff who assist these users. (Of course, not every library patron makes use of this collection, in spite of our attempts to persuade them of its value.) Although there may be some differences in their levels of searching sophistication, both types of users start their search for information in the reference collection because it seems fruitful to do so. That is, the reference collection provides sources that make the search easier or more effective than wading into the main collection. This is a natural consequence of the types of sources located in reference collections.

As discussed earlier, these sources, consisting of ordered files and records, provide faster retrieval of information than other sources. They do this in more than one way. The professional literature usually distinguishes between two types of reference sources: fact sources and "pointers." Fact sources directly provide the information for which a user looks. For example, an almanac will summarize population statistics for the world's nations. Many other types of reference sources have this same fact-source characteristic: atlases, handbooks, encyclopedias, yearbooks, plot summaries, telephone books, CD-ROM compilations of corporations' finances, and so on. The reference file format permits discrete bits of information to be located quickly.

The second type of reference source, the pointer, directs the user to another source, which contains the desired information. These tools are usually called "bibliographic" sources because they provide citations to other publications. Periodical indexes (paper or electronic), bibliographies, and the library's catalog are examples of this kind of source. In most cases, users of bibliographic sources have at least one additional step in their information search than do fact-book users; after identifying a source from a reference tool, they must then locate the referenced item itself. (In some situations, the desired information may be part of the citation itself, and no further looking is required.)

Though the user of a fact book actually retrieves the desired data and the bibliography user must look further, users of both kinds of reference sources are following a similar method: they are using reference sources as *surrogates* for other information sources. Fact sources most often are not publishing their own, new research. Instead, they summarize or abstract information that was originally published in other sources. For example, the *Statistical Abstract of the United States* pulls numeric data out of scores of different U.S. government publications, allowing its users to retrieve a huge amount of information without finding and reading the source publications.

Bibliographic sources also contain surrogates. The surrogate in this case is the bibliographic citation; it stands in for the actual source document it cites. Depending on how the reference source is arranged, the user may obtain not only the identity of a source from this surrogate but also some of its characteristics. These can come from subject headings, classifications, and annotations.

Surrogates for original sources are used when it is easier to consult them than to find the information in the originals. As an example, most people do not create catalogs for their home libraries; the relatively small number of titles, plus the owners' familiarity with them, makes it relatively easy to browse the collection. In contrast, when library collections number in the thousands to millions and users are only infrequent visitors, it becomes necessary to provide an intermediate tool for browsing the collection—the library catalog. Other reference tools are likewise created to facilitate access to these large collections. (Reference tools that serve as finding aids to other reference tools have also become necessary as reference sources have proliferated.)

The nature of the library catalog provides some interesting questions in the current era. Traditionally, the catalog has been one source that refers exclusively to the local collection; it has been a surrogate for that collection alone. Other catalogs in a library refer to materials outside the local library, but these catalogs have been available through other means such as printed volumes in the reference collection or microfiche union holdings. In recent years, a library's online catalog may now include access to any variety of sources that are located physically outside the local library system. For example, the MELVYL system of the University of California provides access to materials in all of the university system's libraries throughout the state: journal article indexes, some with full text; library catalogs of institutions throughout the country; campuswide information systems; freenets; and even weather forecasts. The inclusion of full-text sources on these systems means that some of these sources are *virtually* owned, since they can be viewed or printed just as easily as a book can be viewed or copied. However, system designers must still exercise care in making sure their users can easily determine whether they are searching local holdings only or items that may not be immediately available.

Other reference sources, of course, have always included citations to materials not owned by the local library. By its nature, a reference collection will alert users to the wider information universe. The level at which the local reference collection supports access to this wider world of information will vary with the library's basic philosophy of reference service, which should be part of the reference collection development policy. A major research library, catering to faculty with diverse interests and many graduate students, will attempt to cover as much of the information universe as its budget allows. A small college library, meanwhile, may determine that its students and faculty should primarily use what the local collection contains, and its reference collection may be much smaller and more focused. It may avoid selecting periodical indexes that cover mostly titles not owned locally. Public libraries, which often attempt to provide self-educational opportunities to their typically diverse clientele, have a need for broad coverage in their reference collections as well, but financial limitations and physical space may permit this sort of breadth for only the main library, not smaller branches.

The Importance of a Lean Collection

One should not therefore assume that the larger the collection, the better it serves its users. The whole purpose of the reference collection is to provide surrogates that make the user less likely to wade into the main collection without any idea of where to go. A reference collection that is too large and complex begins to suffer from some of the same problems that make the main collection difficult to use. At the most basic level of functionality, the effective reference collection must follow one of Ranganathan's laws of library science: "save the time of the reader."[8] Select sources that enable the users either to find the information they need or to be directed to the location where it resides. We are all aware of the unusual library patron who wants to search everywhere and enjoys this process, precisely because this sort of user is unusual! However, most users will do as little work as is necessary to obtain what they consider to be a sufficient amount of information. In fact, studies show that people will often prefer information that is less pertinent or even questionable in validity if it is more easily available than the "better" quality information. This phenomenon has led some authors to conclude that a law of "least effort" might best define how people seek and use information.[9]

Thus the aim of reference librarians should be the creation of a reference collection that includes an appropriate number of sources to cover the needs of the majority of its users, so that these users can quickly find brief data or a list of citations to other sources that include the desired data. A collection that is too large will lose its users in its complexity, and one that is too small will lead to frequent failures to answer users' research needs. These users include the reference librarians themselves; in spite of their much greater experience with the collection than patrons, they have frequently created collections that are, as the Biggses write, "too large for thorough exploitation by librarians in the service of information delivery."[10]

Reference collections that are full of deadwood consequently serve their users poorly. An efficient collection will contain few sources that are little used. Studies of circulating collections have revealed that those that are weeded of outdated and infrequently used materials show *increases* in use, in spite of the smaller number of titles.[11] Reasons for this have not been established by research, but reasonable surmises are possible. Newer items appear to get pulled off the shelf in preference to older, less physically attractive sources, no doubt reflecting the users' sense that the more current volumes are more useful or trustworthy. It is highly likely that many users are discouraged when they confront shelves of dusty, unused titles that obscure the most useful titles in the collection. In reference collections, users subsequently turn away from these shelves to the one or two titles they already know, even if these titles are not the most appropriate for their inquiries. What reference librarian at a college library has not tried to wean students from the trusty green volumes of the *Readers' Guide to Periodical Literature*? (Though today the problem is perhaps more often weaning them from a general computer-based index.) Excessive clutter no doubt plays a part here as well. Bookstores encourage general browsing and purchasing by maintaining attractive displays that highlight books rather than hide them, perhaps by turning book covers out to face the browser or creating separate display tables. Supermarkets, another entity with large numbers of products, try to increase usage (that is, purchases) by creating end-of-aisle and free-standing displays that make items stand out from the clutter of the regular shelves. Thus a recently weeded collection may show more useful and interesting titles to the user by eliminating the background clutter of old, uninteresting sources and thereby increase usage of what is then highlighted.

What Belongs in the Reference Collection?

As we have seen, reference sources are used as a simpler and more convenient way of approaching the often vast amount of materials available in a library, either providing summaries and excerpts of the information that may be found in the remainder of the collection or pointing to other sources that will give this information. When titles are evaluated for their usefulness in a library's reference collection, they naturally will be reviewed according to the various criteria pertinent to the type of source as well as the general quality of their execution. These criteria are covered in greater detail in chapters 4 and 5. However, the need for reference sources to provide convenient and quick access to desired information requires that certain characteristics be found in virtually all sources placed in the reference collection. These chosen sources must be

- reference-formatted
- frequently used
- authoritative
- current
- unique in coverage

Reference-Formatted

As noted previously, sources that organize information records into files allow easier and faster consultation than those that contain mainly continuous text. Those without an organized file structure do not belong in the reference collection unless they can provide superior convenience in locating information. This same criterion can apply to nontextual sources, too. For example, an atlas provides not only textual files of place names, population, etc., but also maps that organize geographical data in images.

Frequently Used

Most librarians would admit that their reference collections contain materials that have received little use. In fact, colleagues at other institutions have reported that one method used to weed materials from reference is to measure the dust on top of the volumes. Anecdotal evidence aside, surveys of reference collection use have shown that more than half of most reference collections are not used in any one-year period and as much as one-fourth of the collection is not used over five years.[12] Surely items used less than once per year on a regular basis do not need to occupy space in a collection selected precisely to provide quick and convenient access. These infrequently used volumes become the deadwood that makes searching for valuable resources more difficult. Constance Winchell, a compiler of many reference book lists, reminds us that the "most important element in the equipment of such a department is an adequate and live collection of reference books."[13]

When I discuss these five criteria with other librarians, the one argued about most is frequency of use. Others sometimes argue that the
collection benefits from placing items there that are reference format,
regardless of use, largely because patrons or librarians may be inconvenienced by retrieving the sources from the main stacks—or worse
yet, by not getting to use the sources because they are checked out.

The latter point is easily countered; first, if the sources are likely to
receive very sparing use, they are virtually as likely to be available in
the stacks as they would be in the reference collection. Potential
episodes of inconvenience due to the items being circulated outside
the library will be quite rare. Second, it is quite obvious that a reference volume in use may be inaccessible throughout a day, just as the
circulating volume would be for that same day. Either type of absence
inconveniences users needing information right now.

The more basic argument implies that any owned reference
source by its nature must be in the reference collection and noncirculating. Sometimes this might be applied more moderately to insist that
any "classic" reference source must reside in reference. Yet this argument has not been applied consistently in virtually any library I have
visited. For example, guides to regional information—travel books,
dictionaries of local dialect, Chamber of Commerce publications—are
frequently found in the reference collections of libraries located in
those regions. However, these same publications will frequently be
shelved in the circulating stacks of libraries outside the region, assuming they even purchase the titles. The determining factor here is pro-
jected frequency of use; the libraries outside the region do not expect
a steady number of inquiries requiring the sources, so they are not
placed in their reference collections. In cases where the titles do, in
fact, occur in the distant reference collections, this is usually due to expected popularity. For example, an Orlando, Florida, vacation guide
might be in reference collections throughout the country, but one for
Amarillo, Texas, will likely be declared a reference item mostly in libraries near Amarillo. Thus frequency of use is actually an important
criterion for most libraries, but it is often an implicit assumption. What
is needed is *explicit* and *consistent* application of this principle, both
when a source is selected and when it is reviewed for weeding.

Another argument contends that providing reference sources
about subjects not well-covered in the general collection is a good way
to alert users to a larger world of information that the library has cho-

sen not to collect. The summarization of knowledge found in many reference books makes them very useful for this purpose, as they can less expensively provide brief information on many subjects. Assuming a library offers interlibrary loan services, these reference tools may provide lists of additional resources that can then be acquired.

That these reference-format sources can be excellent purchases for a library cannot be denied, but this in no way requires that they be located in the reference collection. If use is expected to be frequent, then reference is a proper designation. If the subject is so peripheral to normal user needs that only a rare patron uses the secondary source, then that user and the library would benefit more by locating the source in the regular collection where it could be circulated for a longer period and be more convenient for the user.

The criterion of frequent use does present two challenges, however. First, it assumes that librarians can accurately judge or measure how much use these materials receive or are expected to receive. Some limited studies of use have been performed by employing stick-on labels, librarian tallies at the reference desk, and reshelving counts. This problem will be covered in greater detail in chapter 6. In general, when a reference collection is reasonably sized and reasonably staffed, those persons serving the public will usually have a good guess as to which titles are heavily used and which seem to have no demand. (Of course, there is also the "accumulated dust" method.) Second, the frequent use of a source does not mean that the source is necessarily the best one to serve the queries for which it is used. That is, library users may make poor choices when selecting sources on their own. Perhaps they pick books that have more colorful covers or titles that they remember from library visits in the past. Selectors may not agree that a frequently used source warrants the use that it receives from patrons. Once again librarians must balance the importance of what users appear to want with those items that librarians think they should use. It is conceivable that a popular title might be removed from the reference collection if the staff believe that users choose it too often over sources with higher quality information.

Authoritative

As previously mentioned, library users often view items in the reference collection as more authoritative than other sources. Reference librarians, especially in larger libraries, rely mostly on this collection to help the patrons they encounter. Consequently, sources located in reference must be worthy of this reliance. However, some titles make their way into reference collections when they are known to contain errors or their credibility is suspect. A favorite example is the well-known *Gourman Report,* a source that ranks undergraduate and graduate academic programs. Although several scholarly articles and book reviews have questioned its credibility, and librarians are unable to verify the sources of its data and its calculated scores, the title is one of the few ranking sources popularly known and is frequently requested by name. Thus it is shelved in many reference collections, in spite of its known problems. That librarians are uncomfortable with this decision can be seen in frequent discussions of the title, lately found on Internet discussion lists.[14] In light of our knowledge that users will often choose incorrect but convenient information over accurate but inconvenient sources, reference collection selectors must be careful to choose only the most authoritative, trustworthy sources for this collection.

Current

Currency of information is almost always listed as a criterion for reference sources and may seem not worth mentioning. However, those who have looked at the state of reference collections in various libraries have noted that many collections are full of outdated materials, and that librarians appear to rank weeding as one of their most infrequent and disliked tasks.[15] What do we mean when we say that a source is current? A current source is one that provides information that has not yet been superseded. The date of publication by itself does not indicate whether a book is current. A reference book on major communicable diseases compiled in 1980 would be terribly outdated at this point, yet a biographical dictionary of nineteenth-century musicians published in 1980 will probably still be quite accurate and current. The key element here is whether much of the information has changed between the time of publication and the time the source is used.

Of course, rare is the library that can update every reference source as soon as any of it becomes outdated, in part because the time lag between the finishing of a reference work's content and its publication will always allow some obsolescence to occur in even a brand-new work. Budgetary constraints also limit the ability of librarians to replace outdated sources. Therefore, a secondary consideration is the *importance* of currency for the subject. In the earlier example, the use of an outdated medical book could put the user at some health risk, so librarians should be much more diligent about keeping this area up to date. On the other hand, the potential harm appears minor for a patron who misses out on the last ten years of scholarship on a deceased Russian composer. Reference selectors will necessarily need to make subjective judgments on the relative importance of updating and weeding different subject areas.

Once again remember that many, if not most, library users will look to the reference collection for high-quality information. Finding an outdated source, the less-careful user will assume that the information found is valid and trustworthy, unaware that there may be dozens of other books, articles, or Internet sites that could provide more current and accurate information. The librarian may be able to guide the user to more-current sources in some cases, but many users of reference collections do not avail themselves of such services. Thus, it would frequently be better to retain no titles in reference for a particular subject than to include outdated ones.

Unique in Coverage

Sources added to the reference collection should offer a distinctive contribution to locating information within their subject scope. This uniqueness could merely be the greater currency of its information, but more interesting are those sources that fill in voids where previous works provided no assistance. Perhaps additional subjects of study for the discipline have been considered, as seen with the recent proliferation of sources that include women, ethnic minorities, and other groups ignored in earlier scholarship. Perhaps a new treatment of an old topic has been created, or improved indexing has been provided. Many new reference sources have been published in the last several years, but not all of these titles improve on existing sources. Responsible use of collection funds requires reference selectors to justify their purchases, and redundant reference tools may be questionable choices.

Of course, this does not imply that multiple sources on one subject should not be selected. The good titles will all have slight nuances in treatment or coverage that make it worthwhile to compare several for

the same query. Subjects that tend to be discussed from explicitly bi-
ased positions, such as religion, may require the purchase of titles from
a variety of perspectives. Also, heavy demand for sources in a particular
area may require the availability of multiple copies of the same source
or the purchase of alternative sources. However, the collection need not
be cluttered (nor the budget encumbered) by purchasing sources that
add nothing new to what is already there. As Mathews and Tyckoson
point out, "all new reference sources must be better (under one of the
criteria . . .) than the existing titles already in the collection."[16]

Questionable Criteria for Reference Works

A perusal of the professional literature as well as some reference collection policies shows that there are some additional reasons given for
classifying a source to the reference collection. However, careful analysis shows that the following reasons prove insufficient for locating materials in the reference collection.

Requires Instruction by Librarian

Some librarians have indicated that those reference materials that are
difficult for the average patron to use and frequently require a librarian to interpret or explain should be kept in reference. This reasoning
could be compelling for moving items to ready reference areas, where
a librarian should usually be at hand to help. However, frequency of
use should actually determine whether the items ever find their way to
reference. A source that is in a reference format and hard to use, but
rarely used, would need interpretation by a librarian so seldom that it
would merely clutter the reference area's shelves. Many of the materials we collect can be confusing in one way or another to our users, and
though it may be nice to have all the sources near a librarian for consultation, this is not feasible. Again, the reference collection is created
to provide convenience for our users, not to provide an archive.

Protection from Theft or Mutilation

Some library items are at risk of being stolen or having pages ripped
out: local business information, popular fiction, and sexually oriented

materials are typical examples. In many libraries, these higher risk items are frequently relocated to the reference area, where the non-circulating status of the items, plus the watchful eye of a staff member, are thought to provide greater security. However, a reference collection created to enable efficient research and quick fact finding does not function as well when it must dilute its more useful works to become a safe haven for expensive materials—more so when these materials are not even reference sources in format. Most libraries have other locations that can provide security without burdening reference, and those locations would offer better solutions to this problem. Virtually all academic libraries have a reserve collection in which items can be circulated for short-term use, are usually monitored, and are frequently kept in closed stacks. The only drawback to this arrangement is that many reserve collections have limited space at their disposal. Another possible location for many libraries would be their special collections area, which is designed to hold valuable and rare items and receives extensive supervision.

Protection from Circulation

Among those librarians who are uncomfortable with sending virtually any reference-format item to the main stacks, many argue that there are occasions when allowing this type of item to circulate can inconvenience users. In many academic libraries, for instance, faculty members and perhaps graduate students can check out materials for a semester or longer at a time. Though a particular reference source may not be used frequently, these librarians argue, it could too easily be unavailable when that infrequent query arises.

This argument does not survive scrutiny, however. First, any circulating item may be unavailable to a later requester; that does not prevent most libraries from allowing books to be checked out. Additional copies are sometimes provided for the most popular titles, but the vast majority of titles are held in only one copy and may therefore be out of the library when needed. Second, if the title seems important enough to restrict to library use but is unlikely to receive much use, the library may designate the title as "noncirculating" and still place it in the main stacks. Many libraries follow this practice for outdated reference tools, such as back-runs of business statistical handbooks and old periodical index volumes.

Consistency of Location

Consummate organizers that we are, librarians will often want to shelve like sources in like locations. Problems arise when not all similar materials are best suited for reference. For example, one or two monographic bibliographies may be added to a reference collection. Other volumes follow in the same series, and librarians add these new titles automatically to the reference collection. However, the later volumes may or may not reflect subjects for which there is much demand in that library, or they may be inferior in quality to the original volumes. Thus, the titles added automatically because they belong to a series may bloat the collection with unneeded materials. Librarians should instead evaluate each item according to accepted criteria for reference inclusion, including especially the expected use of the new item, and reject those titles not passing this test.

Of course, an exception to this may occur when an ongoing set of titles makes frequent references among its various volumes. For example, large numbers of titles are appearing in the series titled the *Dictionary of Literary Biography.* Each volume covers one particular type of literary author based on genre, nationality, time period, and so on. While some volumes will be heavily used in many libraries, quite a few volumes cover subjects for which demand will be substantially lower. The basic criteria of frequency of use would usually recommend placing these lesser-used titles in the regular collection. However, the set includes extensive cross-referencing from one volume to others, and the most recent volume always indexes the contents of all previous volumes. Thus the utility of having the entire set shelved together in this case probably outweighs the possible inclusion of less desirable titles.

Fills a Niche

Rejecting a source for the reference collection merely because it fills an open niche might sound contradictory to my acceptable criterion of unique coverage, but there is a distinction between the two concepts. Reference librarians, who handle user requests month after month, sometimes note that there is no good reference tool for a particular type of request. A new item that provides coverage for one of these areas is greeted enthusiastically as a good purchase. However, not all of the subject niches in the reference collection need filling. If there is no significant or even occasional user demand for that subject, little need exists for adding it to reference. Selectors must weigh the potential usefulness of a new source against its potential ability to clutter the collection while it sits unused. They can be guided by both the reference collection development policy, which should give some indication of how much collection depth is needed in different subject areas, and their own experience with answering queries from their clientele.

A "Classic" Source

Finally, there are many sources that one or more librarians in a department believe must be in any good reference collection. Some of these tools have earned this reputation due to the frequency with which they perform well in the service of assisting users, and these sources should, of course, be in any collection anticipating similar sorts of user needs. However, some of these sources are considered classics because they were perhaps groundbreaking innovations in reference materials, or maybe they set a standard for accuracy or comprehensiveness that later sources have tried to match. That they are superbly compiled or designed works is laudatory, but this characteristic is not sufficient to automatically insert these titles into every reference collection. Each library's collection serves a different set of users, and a source in heavy demand at one library may gather dust at another. Therefore, the purchase of a title should be driven by the library's overall collection policies, and if the title is anticipated to be used frequently for consultation, only then should it be added to the reference collection.

In summary, figure 1 provides a decision framework for determining whether and where a source should be added to a collection.

The Ready Reference Collection

The physical organization of the reference collection—whether periodical indexes, encyclopedias, and atlases are pulled out of the main sequence and shelved in special areas, for instance—is an interesting

Figure 1.   *Decision Tree for Selecting Reference Sources*

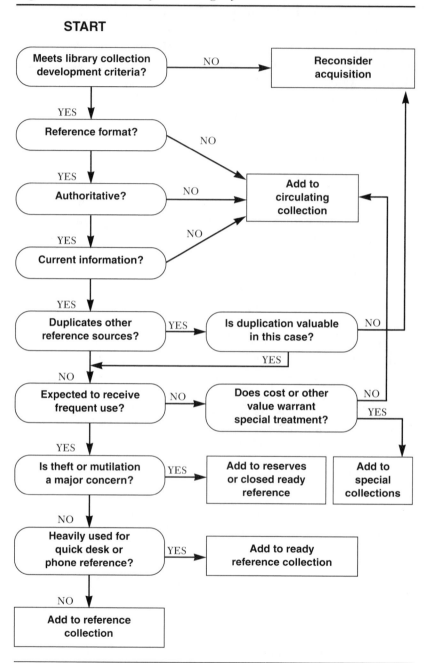

issue that will receive further treatment in chapter 6. However, it may be valuable to attend to one special location that appears in various forms in most libraries—the ready reference collection. This is a special group of reference sources usually located immediately behind or next to the reference desk. In some libraries, ready reference may be a couple of shelves behind the desk. In others, there may be several ranges of shelving with hundreds of titles.

What is the purpose of this collection? As the name indicates, *ready* reference sources are tools that are immediately at hand for a reference librarian's use, just as a writer may wish to have a dictionary, thesaurus, and style guide ready to consult immediately with the smallest disruption of his or her writing. Librarians perceive a number of advantages to creating such a minicollection.

First, one would assume that a reasonable-sized reference collection would be easy enough to consult without the need for a smaller subset of titles. However, many reference collections have become so large that their complexity encourages reference staff to select the better or more frequently needed titles and place them closer to their workspace. Just as the reference collection itself provides a more convenient way to begin searching for information than the main collection, the ready reference titles offer an even more convenient starting point for a select set of common queries.

Second, reference staff are often required to provide assistance to users on the telephone. Unless cordless phones are available, the librarian must leave the phone to consult items in the reference collection. The handy placement of heavily used titles right next to the desk aids the librarian's ability to answer these phone queries.

Third, some library materials are more theft- and mutilation-prone than others, and as noted earlier, these titles are sometimes located in reference for protection. If the normal noncirculating reference collection is seen as placing these desirable items under house arrest, as it were, the ready reference collection often provides a maximum-security detention center. Many ready reference collections are kept in a closed stacks area behind the desk, requiring a librarian to hand an item to a user, often in exchange for a temporarily held identification card. Theft is made much more difficult, and removal of pages is at least discouraged by the possibility that the user's act would be discovered when the title is returned.

Fourth, we cannot dismiss the notion that ready reference collections exist because of an inherent tendency toward "least effort" on the part of the librarian. Many of these ready reference collections have grown quite large, with few titles being withdrawn when new ones are added. The usual reasons given for this are that certain staff are accustomed to finding those old items there without having to walk to the main reference collection and that they would resist any efforts requiring them to find these titles in the reference stacks. Thus, the convenience of the librarian appears to be an important rationale for this smaller collection in terms of physical as well as intellectual effort.

Unfortunately, the existence of the ready reference collection creates some problems, just as it solves others. These problems, many clearly described in Clark and Cary's useful article,[17] include the following:

Fragmentation of the reference collection occurs when some titles are taken out of their normal sequence and moved to the ready reference section. Not all library users go through a reference librarian to locate materials. Some will use the library's catalog; others will browse the reference collection without the catalog. Many will look for these items at odd hours when there are no reference staff on duty. Splitting similar resources among different library locations can confuse patrons. They may look in the main reference stacks, not find the ready reference items, and believe that the sources are missing.

Librarians who have a certain small set of resources at their fingertips will possibly begin to rely on these titles too much, failing to look for sources that are more appropriate for certain queries. (Several colleagues have noted that this is becoming true for electronic resources, which are frequently consulted even when there are superior printed sources available for the problems at hand.)

Librarians fail to browse the reference stacks as frequently, not only denying them the opportunity of learning new titles but also of noting the presence of outdated sources, maintenance problems, and so on.

Librarians who answer too many questions from the ready reference collection have less opportunity for walking through the

reference stacks and using that extra time for considering solutions to the patron's query. Reference interviews can often
be successfully negotiated with the additional dialog that en-
sues during this time. Users who are intimidated at the more
formal reference desk are much more likely to disclose their
actual needs as the conversation moves to a less formal space
away from the desk.

Users who are served exclusively from the ready reference collection may begin to see that collection as the sum of what is important in reference and fail to be introduced to the large
number of other sources that could help them now or in the
future. The users often see the reference librarian as a magi-
cian who reaches back and pulls out the magic source with the
requested information. Pedagogically it is often sounder to allow patrons to view our decision-making processes as we peruse a number of items on the reference shelves and look for
the one that appears most useful.

In spite of these difficulties, the obvious benefits of having some
resources in a ready reference collection make this subset of reference
an important asset to the staff. The problems begin to become more
serious only when ready reference is allowed to become too large. Just
as the overall reference collection should be a trim and active set of resources, so too should ready reference consist of a small number of
heavily used titles. This number can indeed be quite small. In Clark
and Cary's project, ready reference titles were removed to the main
reference collection and brought back only with some justification, a
sort of zero-based selection. An original collection of over two hundred
ready reference titles was reduced to only thirty-four titles.[18]

The criteria for a source's inclusion in the ready reference collection should be quite obvious. Since these titles are a very small selection from the entire collection, they should be expected to provide
maximum utility; that is, they should be expected to receive heavy use
and cover subjects in substantial demand. This may also apply to many
titles in the main reference collection. Additionally, a ready reference
title should be useful to the reference librarian in answering the short,
concrete query for which sources like almanacs, encyclopedias, and
dictionaries are collected. These questions, which usually require a
succinct fact to answer, often arrive via the phone. The small ready

reference collection will be available to provide answers to such questions as the population of a city, the spelling of a word, the address for a university, or the meaning of an acronym. It will permit a rapid location of the desired information without the need for the librarian to leave the desk. Although there is an advantage to walking through the reference collection while working on an interview, there is also an advantage to being able to answer a simple query without removing a staff member from the desk (especially during very busy periods).

The Future of the Reference Collection

This chapter has concentrated on helping selectors determine the best types of resources for a library's reference collection. Electronic sources were mentioned along the way, but much of the discussion related to reference books printed on paper and located in a physical reference collection. Given the rapidly changing environment of digital information today, is this inclusion of the paper-based resources dated?

Although reference sources have a long history, the reference collection is a much newer invention. Katz traced the history of reference sources, noting that compendia of definitions and explanations have been around for thousands of years.[19] During the Middle Ages, libraries chained their valuable sources to the desks, creating a precedent of noncirculation for these items. However, the real growth of reference collections began during the nineteenth and early twentieth centuries, especially in the United States, where the popularity of public libraries brought the general population into their doors and created a need for personal assistance from librarians and printed guides to the libraries' holdings. Thus, Galvin points out, there arose the dictionary catalog, the first periodical indexes, the Dewey Decimal classification, and real reference rooms, which were commonplace by 1893.[20]

The mid-twentieth century saw a large growth in the enrollment in universities and an increasing specialization of knowledge within the different disciplines. As the information in libraries grew rapidly, new reference tools were created to deal with it: specialized indexes and abstracts, national bibliographies for great libraries like the British Museum, and the *National Union Catalog*.[21] From this period through the early 1980s, reference collections continued to add new print-based resources as well as occasional microform titles. Reference rooms contained long rows of periodical index volumes, and most users were required to search through volume after volume if comprehensiveness was their goal.

However, the sheer amount of information being produced was recognized as particularly problematic for researchers in areas such as the space program and medicine. The growing capabilities of the mainframe computer were applied to this problem, and through the efforts of NASA and the National Library of Medicine in the 1960s, online literature searching was created in the form of what later became DIALOG and MEDLINE.[22] Online searching became commonplace in academic, public, and special libraries in the 1970s and 1980s, but the relatively high cost of doing such searches meant that most libraries did not provide the service for the majority of their users. The big change in the presence of electronic reference sources began in the mid-1980s, when first laserdisc and then CD-ROM databases became available to libraries. With unlimited searching for a fixed annual subscription, dozens of periodical indexes became popular in CD-ROM format at libraries of all types. By the late 1990s, thousands of CD-ROM titles are available for purchase or subscription.

The most recent developments have involved the use of the Internet as a method of accessing large databases. Fixed annual subscriptions to a wide variety of databases are available, so that libraries can appropriately budget for them in a way that was difficult for the services of commercial online vendors like DIALOG and STN. The rapid acceptance of the Web and browser software has provided a widespread platform for developing database interfaces, and a considerable number of reference databases can be searched with the same browser interface. The incremental costs of transmitting and receiving data over the Internet are small enough to appear virtually free to libraries, so the accessing of large databases that are stored on remote servers is no longer limited by communications charges. Thus, full-text databases with thousands of articles, illustrations, numeric files, and more are becoming very popular in libraries as the 1990s come to a close.

Library reference sources themselves are now in competition with other resources, both free and fee-based, available on the Web. Indeed, the amount of useful information available freely on the Web has grown dramatically in just a few years (which is not to say that the *percentage* of useful data on the Web has also increased). Librarians and teachers alike will vouch for the frequency with which students expect to find the answer to any question on the Web. Unfortunately, there are also university presidents, legislators, and others in positions of power who make the same comments. The concerns of the reference librarian in this time are twofold: will electronic reference sources drive out print sources, and will the Internet become the reference tool of choice and therefore allow users to bypass the library?

Listening to some pundits, one would think that print as a medium is essentially a dead technology, but a careful glance at the real world shows that paper-based information sources are still going strong. Books and magazines continue to sell well in bookstores. Reference publishers are still producing significant numbers of new works in print to go along with the CD-ROM and Web-based sources; a recent review of the situation assessed the scene for reference titles as "flourishing."[23] The truth is that some types of reference sources, such as periodical indexes, are much easier to use in an electronic format, but others may sometimes be more readable and easier to consult in a print format. Some of these situations in which paper-based sources still outperform electronic sources are presented in chapter 5. Even when electronic products may be more powerful in their capabilities, users can frequently get all the information that they need from the quick use of a book. Also, thousands of titles held in reference collections are not available in electronic format and will not be produced in that format anytime in the foreseeable future.

Print remains a well-refined and often economical method for distributing information. Reference collections will continue to need a mix of formats: electronic, print, sometimes microform or even audiovisual. As Crawford says in his persuasive article, "Paper Persists," the future will have a need for *both* print and electronic, not one or the other.[24] It will be the task of reference selectors to find the best mix of these types of resources for providing effective service to their users while making the most efficient use of the library's funds.

The Internet and the Web will increasingly provide certain types of information to the public, though whether the costs will remain as inconsequential as they currently are is questionable. Thoughts of charging users for the amount of data shipped through their Internet connections have been thrown around for the last few years, and it is conceivable that much of what is freely available now will have costs attached to it in the future. However, make no mistake: users who must come to the library now will find some of what they seek from other sources online. This is not really a radical departure from the past: our users have always used a wide variety of sources for information, and libraries have rarely been the first choice of the majority. As mentioned in chapter 5, librarians can play a role in the use of the Web by using their talents at selection and organization to provide guidance to our clientele. The Web is currently a chaotic collection of data of all qualities, much of it poor quality. Finding those sources that are useful, authoritative, and current will become a major specialty of reference librarians, and our collections will increasingly include both content to which we subscribe and pointers to content held elsewhere over which we have no control. Yet those individuals who value their time and the quality of information they find will resort to libraries for efficient and informed access to this electronic world and to all those resources that remain physically stored in library collections.

Notes

1. Mary Biggs and Victor Biggs, "Reference Collection Development in Academic Libraries," *RQ* 27 (fall 1987): 69–70.

2. David R. Majka, "Reference Collection Maintenance: Theory and (Mal)Practice," *Reference Services Review* (winter 1996): 68.

3. Heartsill Young, ed., *The ALA Glossary of Library and Information Science* (Chicago: American Library Association, 1983), p. 188.

4. For example, see Donald Edward Davinson, *Reference Service* (London: Clive Bingley, 1980), pp. 12–13.

5. Marcia J. Bates, "What Is a Reference Book? A Theoretical and Empirical Analysis," *RQ* 26 (fall 1986): 41–3.

6. Bates, "What Is a Reference Book?" pp. 48–54.

7. Bates, "What Is a Reference Book?" pp. 51–3.

8. M. A. Gopinath, "Ranganathan, Shiyali Ramamrita," in *Encyclopedia of Library and Information Science*, vol. 25 (New York: M. Dekker, 1978), p. 61.

9. Herbert Poole, *Theories of the Middle Range* (Norwood, N.J.: Ablex, 1985), pp. 86–92; Esther G. Bierbaum, "A Paradigm for the '90s," *American Libraries* 21 (Jan. 1990): 18–19; Winifred Sewell and Sandra Teitelbaum, "Observations of End-User Searching Behavior over Eleven Years," *Journal of the American Society for Information Science* 37 (July 1986): 239–40.

10. Biggs and Biggs, "Reference Collection Development," p. 69.

11. Stanley J. Slote, *Weeding Library Collections: Library Weeding Methods,* 4th ed. (Englewood, Colo.: Libraries Unlimited, 1997), pp. 3–5.

12. Biggs and Biggs, "Reference Collection Development," pp. 74–5.

13. Constance M. Winchell, *Guide to Reference Books,* 8th ed. (Chicago: American Library Association, 1967), p. xiv.

14. A useful article on the methods of the *Gourman Report* is David S. Webster, "Jack Gourman's Rankings of Colleges and Universities: a Guide for the Perplexed," *RQ* 25 (spring 1986): 323–31. Discussions of the *Gourman Report's* place in library reference collections were occurring on the Internet list called LIBREF-L during late January–early February, 1998: LIBREF-L Discussion List, online, available LISTSERV@ LISTSERV.KENT.EDU; and a scathing review was written by James Rettig on his "Rettig on Reference" Web site, online, available http://www. gale.com/gale/rettig/199804/colleges.html (13 Apr. 1998).

15. Gail Schlachter, "Obsolescence, Weeding, and Bibliographic Love Canals," *RQ* 28 (fall 1988): 7–8; Eugene A. Engeldinger, "Weeding of Academic Library Reference Collections: A Survey of Current Practice," *RQ* 26 (spring 1986): 367.

16. Eleanor Mathews and David A. Tyckoson, "A Program for the Systematic Weeding of the Reference Collection," in *Weeding and Maintenance of Reference Collections,* ed. Sydney J. Pierce (New York: Haworth, 1990), p. 134; also published as *The Reference Librarian* no. 29 (1990):134.

17. Juleigh Muirhead Clark and Karen Cary, "An Approach to the Evaluation of Ready Reference Collections," *RSR: Reference Services Review* 23 (spring 1995): 39–44.

18. Clark and Cary, "Approach," p. 41.

19. Bill Katz, *Cuneiform to Computer: A History of Reference Sources* (Lanham, Md.: Scarecrow, 1998), pp. 1–5.

20. Thomas Galvin, "Reference Services and Libraries," in *Encyclopedia of Library and Information Science,* vol. 25 (New York: M. Dekker, 1978), pp. 210–26.

21. Galvin, "Reference Services," p. 216.

22. Cindy Faries, "Reference Librarians in the Information Age: Learning from the Past to Control the Future," in *Reference Services Planning in the 90s,* ed. Gail Z. Eckwright and Lori M. Keenan (New York: Haworth, 1994), p. 17; also published as *The Reference Librarian* no. 43 (1994); Emilie V. Wiggins, "National Library of Medicine," in *Encyclo-*

pedia of Library and Information Science, vol. 19 (New York: M. Dekker, 1968), pp. 123–7.

23. Francine Fialkoff, "Reference Is a Mixed Media," *Library Journal* (15 Nov. 1997): S3.

24. Walt Crawford, "Paper Persists: Why Physical Library Collections Still Matter," *Online* 22 (Jan./Feb. 1998): 42–8.

⚉ 2 ⚉

The Reference Collection
Development Policy

Selection is performed by several people at most libraries, who may have similar or dissimilar ideas of what should be collected. They use funds that have been supplied by a university, government, school district, or perhaps corporation. Those who supply the funds occasionally want to know how the funds have been used to see if the money has been spent for the proper materials. Libraries have traditionally created collection development policies to provide information about their selection activities. There are probably few libraries that do not have some form of policy about their general collections. However, the Biggses' survey in the late 1980s found that few libraries had constructed policies for their reference collections: while nearly 60 percent of Association of Research Libraries institutions had policies, only 17 percent of masters-level libraries and 7 percent of undergraduate institution libraries had such a policy for reference materials.[1]

Rationale for the Policy

The number of articles focusing on the management of the reference collection that have been published in subsequent years shows the concern that this situation elicited from reference librarians, and the percentage of libraries without a reference collection policy is no doubt much lower today than in the previous decade. The tightening of library budgets and the justification required for selecting expensive reference sources have also played a part in this development.

As Johnson points out, collection development policies are principally documents for communication with external users and internal staff.[2] Library users (and funding sources) are given information about the types of subjects and materials the library collects and the clientele for whom the materials are selected as well as which materials are not collected. Of course, this policy should be created with the needs of the library's users as the foremost priority; the goals of the selection process should not be created in isolation from considerations of the needs of the primary users. The collection policy also serves as a way to inform these user groups what the library cannot do, helping to ensure that potential controversies are avoided. The library cannot select every item any user might want, and the policy provides a rationale for not selecting certain types of materials. In this way, the policy protects the library and its staff. Richards and Eakin note that the policy also protects the interests of those users who are less vocal in their demands than other users by providing a systematic collecting plan, not just a reaction to immediate demands.[3]

The collection development policy also guides library staff in the selection process. Many staff are often involved in selection activities, and there needs to be a consensus about the end results of their work. A policy document that has been discussed and written by staff provides a framework for consistency in collection development. Questions about who is responsible for certain subjects and formats can be answered, expectations about what growth is considered appropriate in these areas can be established, and overly individualistic interpretations of the library's policies can be minimized.[4] The policy can later serve as a standard to which the staff or others can point when attempting to evaluate the quality of collection management.

Critics have sometimes opposed the idea of creating separate reference collection development policies. Batt makes the case that these policies seldom appear to have any effect on the daily collection activities of reference librarians; once written, they are rarely consulted again. He also believes that the collection is most effectively evaluated through its daily use by librarians and patrons and that policies therefore contribute little to the assessment of the reference collection.[5] He does not oppose a general collection development policy for the library, merely a separate one for reference.

The criticism that these policies may go unused by the reference librarians is probably somewhat accurate; most of us would say that this situation rings true not only for this but also for many of the other policies that a library creates. However, the purpose of such a policy is not to require daily or weekly referral to it for normal staff activities. The document is created to provide a consensus among the staff about the major goals for the reference collection and the ways in which those goals are to be achieved. Because of staff turnover or even just staff forgetfulness, the creation of a collection development policy in concrete form provides something tangible for referral when problems arise or when the collection is being assessed. As Evans notes, "a written policy helps assure continuity and consistency in the collecting program despite changes in staff and funding."[6]

In particular, the reference collection development policy is important because of the special nature of the collection. As discussed in chapter 1, the reference collection is a special working collection for librarians and users, one that operates best if certain types of materials are included in and others are excluded from it. Inattention to the reference collection has resulted in some libraries providing outdated sources that hinder their users and reflect badly on the entire library.

Elements of the Policy

At a minimum, librarians should include a special section in their overall library collection development policies indicating the types of materials that the reference collection should contain, the criteria used to determine when items belong in reference, and how the collection will be managed and assessed. The following section provides some guidance on what the more full-bodied reference collection development policy might contain. The assumption is that most libraries will include such a policy as one part of the overall library collection development policy. For those libraries without such a comprehensive policy, reference selectors should at least create a separate one for their area of responsibility.

Introduction

The introductory section of the policy should relate the ensuing document to the library's overall collection development plan. That is, there should be a reminder of the clientele being served and the general aims of the library's collections. There is no need for the reference policy to spend a great deal of space repeating the overall mission and values listed in the overall library policy. However, it is helpful if the reference librarians create a statement that indicates the functions they see the reference collection serving for their particular library. For example, though an academic library may not generally collect any materials for users other than students, faculty, and staff, the reference collection may well serve a large number of other community users. The reference policy should indicate whether any materials are purchased to support these general users or whether funds are expended only for the primary user groups. As another example, in the current era, more and more users are accessing library reference sources electronically from outside the library. These remote users sometimes require different types of sources and services than those users in the library. The policy should indicate whether the reference collection will support these users as fully as in-person users or if these users are considered secondary to those physically within the library.

The introduction to the policy should also contain some overarching ideal of what the reference collection should contain. Chapter 1 made a case for supplying the reference collection solely with authoritative sources that are likely to be frequently used. If the library staff agrees with this view, then the collection development policy should indicate it. On the other hand, if the reference department thinks it is more valuable to house all reference-format materials in the reference collection regardless of their use, then this has a definite impact on how the collection is built and managed. That view should likewise be included in the introduction.

Scope

The general policy for the entire library will indicate the scope or the types of subjects that will be supported by the library as well as the formats that will be acquired. The reference policy does not need to repeat these statements. Instead, the reference policy will be more useful if it highlights any differences between the general collection policy and that for reference. For example, a certain library may decide that it does not collect materials to support genealogical work, but the reference selectors may decide to purchase occasional reference sources that can help users find out which other libraries may be helpful for this research.

Also helpful in the policy's statement of scope is any delineation of boundaries for collecting among various libraries in a multilibrary environment. On academic campuses, a main reference collection may include only the most basic sources in a subject area for which there is a branch library. In a public library system, some of the branches may be intended to provide only a certain level of collection in many areas, relying on the central branch to carry the more comprehensive collection in those subjects. This type of decision, entered into the text of the policy, helps to avoid unnecessary duplication and clarify what the different libraries' selectors are responsible for acquiring.

A key point in the policy is a description of the comprehensiveness with which the library approaches the materials that fall outside the general boundaries of the general collection policy. As was mentioned in chapter 1, the reference collection is first a summary of and an index to the other information in the library collection. The bibliographic tools especially serve as an entrance to the range of materials in the library's main collections. However, bibliographic tools are rarely limited to just what is held in one library's collection; they usually cover some part of all available information that is "out there" in the larger world. A reference collection can focus on the use of local materials, thereby concentrating on tools that highlight the sources owned by that library, or it can broaden its focus by acquiring materials that point to many sources outside the local library collection. For instance, a small college library may subscribe to indexes that cover basic English-language periodical sources that are most likely to be held locally; the Wilson indexes are often good for this purpose. Conversely, the library may decide that it wants to encourage use of the wider world of information by its students, and therefore it will subscribe to more-comprehensive indexes that will encourage students to seek materials through interlibrary lending or document delivery. There are pedagogical arguments for both approaches and budgetary ones as well. Whichever approach the library selectors want to pursue, it should be clearly stated in the reference collection development policy.

A major concern today is deciding where the reference collection actually ends. In earlier decades, the reference collection was a physical collection of materials that were housed in particular locations. Although librarians may have wanted to provide information about the entire realm of knowledge, the limitations of budget and space prevented that reality. Today, the advent of the Internet has dramatically opened up the boundaries of the reference collection. All sorts of people and organizations are placing information that has reference value on servers that can be accessed by anyone with a communications connection and a computer. Certainly, many of these sources are not authoritative, high-quality reference tools. Yet there are significant numbers of sources that do provide timely, dependable information. Avoidance of these "titles" as sources for the reference collection seems shortsighted; if they can serve the needs of our users, they are sources that we should attempt to collect. The reference collection development policy should provide some indication of how much of this new world of data the library's selectors think they should attempt to offer to their clientele.

Finally, selectors may wish to state some indication of the collection's optimal size, at least in terms of materials physically located in the department. Often, this factor is included out of necessity—some reference departments have run out of room for any more print volumes in their reference areas. (Unfortunately, some libraries fail to weed the collection regularly to prevent this sort of occurrence.) If physical space is a serious concern, selectors can state this problem in the policy. However, it seems improbable that the quality of a reference collection can be judged on how well it fills a particular library space. Instead, selectors should consider the merits of maintaining the leanest collection that does the job properly and aim for that qualitative goal rather than any volume count.

Staff Responsibilities

The policy requires a description of staff assignments for reference collection management. Different libraries use a variety of methods to select and weed reference sources; several models are presented in chapter 3. Since the reference collection is a working tool of the reference staff, they have a vested interest in the makeup of that collection. As a result, decisions must be made on whether subject specialists, reference librarians as individuals, a committee of librarians, the head of reference, or some other staff grouping is responsible for selecting reference sources. The institutionalization of this responsibility avoids a situation in which no one is sure who should be selecting reference materials, allowing some sources to be missed that should have been acquired.

Selection

Many reference collection development policies include an explanation of the criteria used for acquiring sources. Batt points out that most of these are self-evident; which library intentionally selects materials that are out-of-date or are of questionable authority?[7] Thus he argues that most of these are unnecessary and a waste of time. What this critique fails to realize, however, is that not all reference selectors agree on what constitutes a good reference source. The policy-creation process is not one that must take a long time or must be re-done frequently. It is something that can be pursued over some number of weeks, allowing staff to build a consensus on the types of materials they think will provide the best service to their users. Certainly, acquiring only authoritative reference sources, for instance, seems self-evident. Yet if this were true and selectors always followed this criterion, then why would many collections contain an obviously controversial source such as the *Gourman Report*? Instead, the discussion of these criteria among reference selectors and their incorporation into the policy will at least provide some increased focus by the selectors on the criteria they should be considering with every purchase.

The next section found in many reference policies is a statement of the materials that are collected within the various categories of reference sources. The most common divisions of reference materials include almanacs and yearbooks, annual reviews, bibliographies, biographical sources, concordances, corporate annual reports, dictionaries, directories, encyclopedias, geographic sources, handbooks, indexes and abstracts, legal materials, library catalogs, plot summaries, sacred books, standards, statistics, style manuals, and telephone books.[8] The materials section of the policy is also sometimes used as the outline for discussing the selection of materials by subject. That is, a selector may describe the materials acquired in the area of history by delineating the types of dictionaries, bibliographies, and other sources that would be acquired in this subject. The section on materials is often too detailed in many policies; it can be assumed that the general collection development policy for the library will cover the intensity of collecting and the subject areas that will be acquired within each discipline.

More useful for the reference policy is a listing of any exceptions to the general policy. For instance, the library's general policy may list travel materials as something not generally collected by the library. The reference selectors, however, may decide that a certain number of these guides are useful in answering reference questions, and so this fact is entered into the reference policy. Under the heading of "dictionaries," it would be obvious to state that an American library will collect basic and comprehensive English-language dictionaries. Instead, a more useful note in this section of the policy would be a mention of whether multiple copies of basic dictionaries are made available, or whether, for languages not supported in the general collection, there is an attempt to acquire a dictionary or two for the reference collection.

Special Policies

The reference collection development policy should contain descriptions of any materials or processes for which special procedures may need to be followed. Typically, this will include statements on the desirability of duplication in the collection or among collections (including which materials will be duplicated in different branch libraries), special retention decisions for materials such as directories and annual statistical compendia, and evaluation and weeding statements. Elements for many of these special policies are covered in chapter 6. Reference librarians may wish to include most of the procedural matters in a separate reference department procedures notebook, rather than the collection development policy. This is mostly a matter of preference; there is no reason to avoid including it in the reference policy, unless one is attempting to keep the policy section as streamlined as possible.

One area for which a special policy seems mandated is that of electronic resources. How does a library collect materials on the Web? These electronic sources are ephemeral: appearing, changing, and disappearing without notice. The normal acquisitions filters of publishers and reviewers are not in place for these electronic sources. Many librarians have begun attempts to catalog items on the Internet, but the task is daunting. How can a library staff, which may have been just adequate to provide bibliographical control to the thousands or tens of thousands of print items received in a year, monitor and catalog the hundreds of thousands of Internet sites? Some additional thoughts on the selection of Internet resources are found in chapter 5.

Although the ideal way of treating these materials is mainstreaming them into the library's normal procedures, as Demas and others so cogently argue, even they recognize that selecting these materials is not second nature to us at this point.[9] Norman's excellent survey article describes many of the important points that must be addressed for the selection of electronic products, points that are not usually necessary when considering traditional materials:

> special budgeting (such as whether money should be taken from the central line or subject lines of a library's budget)
> locus of decisions (often the director or dean is involved in electronic purchases, unlike the case with most print sources)
> methods for evaluating the suitability of electronic sources, including a list of "emerging criteria" that supplement the traditional criteria for library materials
> new considerations for weeding and replacing print titles with electronic
> new roles for collection development librarians[10]

Johnson states that the presence of these additional considerations for selecting electronic resources suggests that a separate document may be written on these sources.[11] However, electronic resources must be evaluated in terms of the library's overall mission and goals, just as other reference sources should be. Most libraries have not received major supplements to their budgets to acquire the new electronic products; these sources compete for the same funds as other library materials. Hence, the optimal treatment of electronic sources is the inclusion of them in the other library collection development policies.

Nonreference types of digital sources should be discussed in the general library policy; electronic reference tools should be discussed in the reference policy (or that section of the general policy devoted to reference materials). Certainly the major differences between print and electronic products need to be considered, but the majority of traditional points considered before acquiring a print source are still valid. (See chapter 4 for a discussion of the traditional selection criteria and chapter 5 for a special discussion of additional concerns for electronic products.)

Budget

The reference policy should describe the way funds are provided for the purchase of reference sources. There are many methods that libraries can use to allocate funds; Richards and Eakin mention budgeting by discipline, academic department, type of material, and location as just a few.[12] It is highly preferable that a separate budget line be established for reference sources regardless of the personnel who actually select for the collection. When reference materials must be purchased out of general subject lines, there is often a tendency for selectors to favor general collection materials over reference materials. This problem is exacerbated when a reference title is expensive and multidisciplinary. No selector may want to commit a large portion of his or her subject budget to a source that is relevant to many other subjects; as a result, some purchases fall through the cracks and are never made. Some libraries may wish to keep most of the budget money in subject lines but place a smaller amount in a reference line. This procedure will at least provide some funds to cover those purchases that are not picked up by any of the subject specialists. The reference policy should indicate the parts of the budget from which major reference purchases are to be made and the staff responsible for doing this. Some other budgetary issues in terms of the staff doing the selection of reference sources are discussed in chapter 3.

External Relationships

The external relationships section of the collection development policy should spell out the library's position on working with other libraries for reference collection support. This can include a consortium in which libraries may share the purchase of electronic reference sources, for instance, or a cooperative agreement in which one library will acquire and maintain sources in one particular subject area while yielding collection responsibility for a different area to another library. The latter situation need not be formalized; libraries in the same geographic area have often done this sort of resource sharing informally. Of course, if one library fails to live up to an informal agreement, there is little that can be done by the other partners. The reference collection policy may also indicate the presence of any cooperative arrangements in which a library agrees to serve as a second resort when a local library cannot help its users. For example, many public libraries belong to cooperative systems in which a regional library center provides backup reference service for member libraries. The regional library may own many of the more expensive titles that the smaller, local reference collections cannot afford. Noting this arrangement in the reference collection development policy helps local staff decide the level of selection that is most appropriate for their collections.

Creating the Policy

If no reference collection development policy exists, librarians who would like to write one will first need to get the support of those to whom they report. These types of policy documents carry no real weight unless the administration of the library puts its authority behind them. In many academic libraries, the approval of the library director is certainly a minimum, and often sufficient, requirement. Smaller academic libraries may need to take the issue further, receiving the support of the college administration. School libraries and public libraries, of course, usually report to some sort of governing board that is located beyond the library. Any prolonged challenges to the selection of reference materials will ultimately be directed to these bodies, so these groups should at least have a general interest in the creation of such a policy before the library selectors go into any detailed work.

The actual development of the policy should be undertaken by a group of librarians and, in some cases where public involvement is especially critical, representative library users. If the size of the reference staff is appropriate for a functional committee, the entire department may draft the first document, perhaps assigning different sections to different subgroups. In larger organizations, an entire department may be unwieldy, and a smaller committee should be chosen. Some thought should be given to including members from outside the reference department. For example, a medium-sized academic or public library may include a member from the cataloging department; a large academic library may include subject bibliographers who do not work in the reference department. As many of the following chapters emphasize, the successful management of a reference collection requires the cooperation of many staff outside the reference department. Therefore, the inclusion of members from these affected departments in the drafting of the document will create goodwill with those departments, and it will have the concrete effect of avoiding problems that are more obvious to these external members.

Of course, many reference collection policies have already been written by other libraries and are available to the public. A quick way to begin the process would be to view a number of policies and find one upon which to build and revise. Often they are found as sections of larger collection policies. Recent books with good examples of reference collection policies include those of Evans and Futas.[13] Watson compiled a collection of reference policies, which included reference collection development policies, though it is a bit dated now.[14] Many libraries have put their collection development policies out on the Web; a search engine will retrieve a number of these documents. Also on the Web is a collection of representative policies for electronic sources gathered by the Collection Development Policies Committee of the Collection Development and Evaluation Section of ALA.[15]

Notes

1. Mary Biggs and Victor Biggs, "Reference Collection Development in Academic Libraries," *RQ* 27 (fall 1987): 70–1.

2. Peggy Johnson, "Collection Development Policies and Electronic Information Sources," in *Collection Management for the 21st Century: A Handbook for Librarians*, eds. G. E. Gorman and Ruth A. Miller (Westport, Conn.: Greenwood, 1997), p. 84.

3. Daniel T. Richards and Dottie Eakin, *Collection Development and Assessment in Health Science Libraries*, vol. 4 of *Current Practice in Health Sciences Librarianship*, ed. Alison Bunting (Lanham, Md.: Medical Library Association and Scarecrow Press, 1997), p. 57.

4. Richards and Eakin, "Collection Development," pp. 57–8.

5. Fred Batt, "The Detailed Reference Collection Development Policy: Is It Worth the Effort?" in *Evaluation of Reference Services,* ed. Bill Katz and Ruth A. Fraley (New York: Haworth, 1984), pp. 313–19. Also published as *The Reference Librarian,* no. 11 (1984): 313–19.

6. G. Edward Evans, *Developing Library and Information Center Collections,* 3d ed. (Englewood, Colo.: Libraries Unlimited, 1995), p. 78.

7. Batt, "The Detailed Reference Collection Development Policy," p. 319.

8. This list was taken from Elizabeth Futas, *Collection Development Policies and Procedures,* 3d ed. (Phoenix: Oryx, 1995).

9. Samuel Demas, Peter McDonald, and Gregory Lawrence, "The Internet and Collection Development: Mainstreaming Selection of Internet Resources," *Library Resources & Technical Services* 39 (July 1995): 275–90.

10. O. Gene Norman, "The Impact of Electronic Information Sources on Collection Development: A Survey of Current Practice," *Library Hi Tech* 15, no. 57/58 (1997): 123–32.

11. Johnson, "Collection Development Policies," pp. 86–7.

12. Richards and Eakin, "Collection Development," pp. 159–65.

13. Evans, *Developing Library and Information Center Collections,* and Futas, *Collection Development Policies and Procedures.*

14. *Reference Policy and Administrative Documents,* ed. Paula D. Watson (Chicago: American Library Association, 1985).

15. Collection Development and Evaluation Section, American Library Association, "Collection Development Policies Committee," online, available http://academic.uofs.edu/organization/codes/begin.html (5 May 1998).

ঙ 3 ৩

Selectors for the
Reference Collection

The choices of materials that go into a library's reference collection are important decisions because the quality of the library's reference services will depend on that collection. Consequently, the question of who is responsible for the selection, maintenance, and weeding of these sources is itself an important issue to consider.

Who will select for the reference collection is not always a straight-forward issue because this collection differs from the main library collection in ways that affect selection. For instance, reference collections may attempt to cover areas of knowledge beyond what the library normally obtains for its main collections; perhaps some attempts are made to provide basic information for subjects in which the library cannot afford to purchase much material. These "fringe" subjects may fall outside the normal responsibilities of the library's selectors, and someone must take on these areas.

Perhaps more importantly, libraries most often divide up selection responsibilities according to subject areas or media formats. Thus one selector may collect business and economics sources that appear as monographs or serials, while another selector may purchase audiovisual materials in these and other areas. Occasionally, some confusion could occur over whose subject a particular source falls into, leading to sources mistakenly not being purchased because one selector assumed another selector would buy those items. The media formats are more obvious, and the responsibility to purchase videotapes or audio compact discs is usually quite clearly defined.

Reference sources, however, are chosen for characteristics that are not included in these usual divisions of labor. Once an item is deemed suitable for a library's collection because of its subject and its medium, determination of its suitability for reference is initially judged on whether it is formatted as a reference source, and then by the other criteria that were discussed in the first chapter. Thus the selection of reference sources requires that another layer of decision be made that cuts across subject and media lines. Careful consideration should therefore be given to which staff in the library are best suited for selecting and determining the location for reference materials.

The following sections look at several models for determining who makes the selection and maintenance decisions for reference sources, paying attention to the library situations in which these models are most used, the advantages and disadvantages of using those models, and especially what actions can be taken to ameliorate any disadvantages. The models are divided into those in which any number of individual selectors have the major responsibility for developing the collection on their own (a distributed model) and those in which a group of librarians makes decisions within a cooperative arrangement. Note that the choice of a model for a particular library is often based on several factors, not just the choice of the best theoretical decision-making model. Some libraries have limited staffing or must deal with allocations of staff that make some models more difficult to implement; other libraries must face political realities concerning who has traditionally had the authority to make reference collection decisions; and yet other libraries may assign responsibilities based on the talents of their current employees. Increasingly, some libraries are finding that the expensive electronic products to which they subscribe are most cheaply purchased through a consortium of libraries; decisions then need to be agreeable to the entire consortium and are therefore often made at a level far above that of a local reference department.

Distributed Selection

When selection is distributed among many selectors, they are usually each assigned a particular subject or discipline. However, they usually select for their own areas without needing permission or input from the other selectors. In many libraries, this distributed method assigns responsibility to groups of librarians, such as subject bibliographers or reference librarians. Occasionally, librarians from several different departments will receive these assignments, although it is more common for them to be all from one department. Of course, in small libraries, the selection responsibility may be given to one individual.

Subject Bibliographers

Many large libraries, especially academic research libraries, employ several professionals as subject bibliographers. These librarians are usually members of the collection development staff, not reference librarians. Very often possessing advanced degrees in their subject specialties, subject bibliographers are responsible for a majority of the library's selection of new materials regardless of the specific collection in which the materials are eventually shelved. They usually have a first-rate knowledge of publishers' offerings in their subjects.

When subject bibliographers are responsible for selecting items for the reference collection, the collection benefits from the skill of these staff in locating any reference sources that might be available. These staff are especially strong in locating bibliographic reference tools in their specialties, including many that may be missed by simply following approval plans and publishers' sales catalogs and brochures. Subject bibliographers also provide continuity between purchases for the reference and the main collections because the same person makes decisions for both.

However, there are drawbacks to using this approach. Kroll points out that a certain "tunnel vision" may occur: When a bibliographer focuses intently on a particular subject and on acquiring everything appropriate in it, the service implications of that collecting activity are missed.[1] When a title is suggested for addition to the reference collection, a subject bibliographer is well-equipped to determine whether it is reference-formatted, authoritative, and current. However, this librarian usually does not have the daily interactions with library users to know how much use the title is likely to receive or the knowledge of what questions have been inadequately answered by the collection in the past; therefore, he or she cannot judge what new sources are needed to fill that gap. The general tendency of this style of reference selection toward comprehensiveness can lead to a collection that grows too large. Kroll posits the circumstance in which the bibliographer creates a well-balanced and in-depth reference collection based on an ideal model of what the collection should be, but that is divergent from the realities of changing patron use patterns.[2] Stebelman also points out that the lack of a separate line for reference purchases could, in fact, lead a subject specialist to spend more freely on monographs for the circulating collection than on reference books for the same subject.[3]

If we agree that the reference collection should consist of a lean, efficient set of resources, then this model of collection development does not rate as the best alternative. On the other hand, for libraries in which this model is established, there are ways for the model to work better. Some bibliographers in large academic libraries maintain contact with the faculty of their subject departments, which provides them with the possibility of at least some awareness of what faculty and students might be requesting. In addition, bibliographers could spend some time learning more about patron use of the reference collection from the reference staff by observing on a regular basis, attending occasional reference meetings, or discussing the collection with the staff.[4]

A more formal method might be to create procedures that allow reference librarians to give feedback on any potential reference titles. For example, bibliographers who have ordered items for reference could have the materials placed on shelves periodically for reference librarians to review. Just as many libraries have slips of paper for recommendations from faculty on approval books, recommendation slips could be placed in the reference titles for comments from reference librarians. This permits reference staff some input into the process without necessarily removing the organizational authority for these decisions from the subject bibliographers.

Reference Librarians

In many libraries, reference librarians select materials for the reference collection in subject areas they have been assigned to cover; rather than many of the staff consulting on various sources, each librarian selects titles as an individual activity. There are at least two models of collection development in which reference librarians individually select for the reference collection. In the first, these librarians are assigned particular subject areas of the reference collection to develop, but they do not have collection development responsibilities for the main collection. This is again more common in large research libraries, academic or public, in which other bibliographers are on the staff. The second model is one in which reference librarians are assigned subjects for which they collect all sorts of resources for any of the library's collections, including reference.

The benefits of these models are quite obvious. Those librarians who interact directly with the library's user population and answer their questions are able to select materials reflecting the users' expressed needs. Reference librarians use reference tools on a daily basis and are best able to determine whether a source provides the utility that it should. Well-designed sources that unfortunately serve no regular need in reference can be located elsewhere, keeping the collection lean. Changes in what users need may be picked up quickly at the reference desk, allowing staff to consider revising their collection development policies to match their new environment.

The major advantages of having reference librarians as selectors can hide some of the drawbacks, but they do exist. Librarians who perform no other collection development may be relatively less informed about publishing in their assigned areas, thus possibly missing out on the selection of sources that are not available through the most obvious distribution channels. Those that do have these extra collecting duties frequently combine them with reference work and library instruction for their assigned subjects, often being called "liaison librarians."[5] This combination of reference work with collection development duties can be quite time-consuming and can lead to difficulties in maintaining all duties equally. Since the patron at the reference desk and the class requiring instruction have an immediacy that book ordering does not, reference collection development can become an afterthought at times. Not only does purchasing new materials receive less attention than it might, but there is very little time spent on maintenance and weeding activities.

Additionally, dividing the collection responsibilities among several reference librarians who work individually, with no oversight from others in the department, can lead to inconsistency in following

the department's collection policy and the possibility of letting multi-
or interdisciplinary resources fall through the cracks.[6] Unless this individual spends a great deal of time at the reference desk or otherwise in contact with users, it is difficult to get a full grasp of the range
of questions that users bring to the library. In many academic libraries, the average time spent at a reference desk in any given week
is twelve to fifteen hours.[7] Although years of experience build up a
good knowledge of typical user needs, shared perceptions from a
group of reference staff always contain a fuller picture than that of
any single librarian. It is possible for the one selector to omit the acquisition of some reference sources based on his or her lack of experience with questions in those areas. Once again, the way a library
provides for better selection in this situation is to encourage contin-
ual feedback from the other reference staff to the one making the selection and deselection decisions.

When reference librarians do not perform collection development
for the main collection and this responsibility resides with bibliographers, the reference staff's lesser knowledge of the collection and the
publishing world can be supplemented by that of the bibliographers.
The full-time selectors can take it upon themselves to forward notices
of potentially useful reference sources that the reference librarians
might miss. The more formal procedure of creating reference decision
shelves, described previously, would also work well in this situation.
However, rather than having the bibliographers make the final decision, the reference librarians could each indicate whether the titles
preselected by the bibliographers should be cataloged as reference titles or not.

The issue of split responsibilities for liaison librarians and the resultant lack of attention given to the reference collection are more difficult problems. Human nature will dictate that those tasks that seem
less urgent and immediate will be postponed in favor of those with the
most immediacy, and reference collection management rarely pos-
sesses a strong sense of urgency. Collection additions will fit in well
with most other collection development done by the reference librarians, so new titles from approval plans and those advertised by major
publishers will be considered within a reasonable time. However, the
literature shows that reference collection maintenance and weeding
are infrequently and sporadically attempted. Successful integration of
these activities into the workflow of liaison librarians will be aided by

an effort to schedule the activities on a regular basis so that staff will be able to gauge how much or little of these needs have been met. A better solution is to have someone provide oversight for this process and be responsible for checking on progress in these activities and coordinating their regular completion.

Head of Reference or Reference Collection Coordinator

One of the most popular models consists of either the head of the reference department or a designated reference coordinator doing all or most of the selection. This person monitors arrivals on the library's approval plan, coordinates all the firm orders placed for reference materials, and has sole responsibility for managing the reference collection budget. Maintenance issues, including periodic weeding, may also be included in these responsibilities. As with individual reference librarians as selectors, this position may include other collection development assignments for the main collection, or it may be limited to just reference materials decisions.

The most obvious advantage of this arrangement is that a person knowledgeable about the daily encounters between librarians and library users makes the choices of materials. Few problems should exist with seldom-used materials being added to the collection. There is also the likelihood of a greater level of consistency in building and maintaining the collection when only one person performs these tasks. A single coordinator of the collection should be able to sense how well balanced the reference collection is and, being aware of his or her need to manage the entire collection, will be less likely to ignore those materials that do not fit neatly into just a single discipline, such as multidisciplinary encyclopedias and bibliographies.

Part of the advantage of this situation is that the single reference selector, who has been given a budgeted amount for these sources, will not have the tendency to ignore the purchase of a source based solely on its subject area. This librarian is much more likely to purchase items based on what would best work for the queries and needs of the users. On the other hand, with many selectors of reference sources having their own subject lines in the budget, there is always a chance that one selector will pass on a source with the hope that another selector will choose it and encumber the money from that person's funds. This situation is most likely to occur when the collection budget is perceived as very tight and a selector cannot purchase many of the desired sources.

Cataloging Staff

One additional way in which libraries assign individual responsibility for reference collection development is to give this task to staff in technical services, most often the cataloging department. When this model is implemented, the decision to add a source to the reference collection usually occurs when the source is being cataloged. A new book or serial is evaluated based on whether its format is that of a reference book. If so, the title is cataloged for a reference location.

There is a good chance that most materials that are truly formatted as reference sources will be identified as such by cataloging staff; as Bates pointed out in her empirical study, the vast majority of publications are predominantly either continuous text or arranged files and records—there are few titles with relatively equal proportions of both.[8] Since cataloging departments will process all of the materials entering the collection, they should be able to catch virtually all materials that are likely candidates for reference.

Of course, the drawback to this model is similar to that of having subject bibliographers do the choosing for the reference collection: staff who do not directly serve the public are less familiar with what materials are necessary to support the library's reference functions. Although an experienced cataloger is probably quite aware of the emphases of the library's collection building, that cataloger is not in a position to know whether the same areas generate much activity at the reference desk or whether a particular source is arranged in such a way that it has substantial usefulness for reference librarians. Consequently, a library that gives decision-making authority to its catalogers for the placement of sources into the reference collection must use methods identical to the ones listed for subject bibliographers: Allow catalogers the chance to become familiar with reference desk activity, to monitor what is reshelved from the collection, to attend at least occasional reference department meetings, and perhaps even to serve at the reference desk on a periodic basis; or establish a system where reference staff can indicate their recommendations and preferences for the location of new titles entering the library.

Cooperative Selection

Another technique followed in some libraries is the assignment of reference collection decisions to a group of librarians, the ubiquitous library committee. In some ways, these are attempts to bridge the downside characteristics of having all reference selectors working individually or of having only one person designated as the reference selector. Public library situations often require the use of committees in which a central group determines what is needed for the many branches; school media centers also may require a committee, where the selection of materials for children undergoes a more rigorous screening than that required for an academic library.

Committee of Reference Librarians

All of the reference librarians in the department may serve together as a reference collection selection committee. In some cases this can be implemented by allowing committee members to work on different parts of the collection according to subject, then bringing their recommendations to the entire committee for approval. Perhaps more common in large libraries is the scenario in which a few selected reference librarians are appointed to a reference sources committee; again, subject areas are usually divided among committee members who report their recommended purchases to the group. This model may be a little less common for decisions about monographs, but it appears to be used frequently for serials sources. Serials, based on their ongoing publication nature and the attendant commitment to annual subscriptions, have become much more heavily scrutinized sources in today's cost-conscious libraries. Thus many libraries have procedures that require a new reference serial to be discussed at a meeting and voted upon by the committee members. (This method is even more popular when electronic indexes and databases are under consideration; this will be investigated in a later chapter.)

These methods positively involve the expertise of the reference staff in the decision-making process and can lead to more-deliberative choices for the collection. The advantages in allowing several librarians to consult on a choice are considerable. However, the principal drawback is the amount of time it can take to make decisions on all these choices. Due to the continued plethora of sources available every year, the number of sources that must be considered can be quite large. Naturally, group decision making can frequently take more time than that of an individual. Therefore, it may be necessary to find ways to streamline this process if a reference committee is the desired model of selection. These can include

> dividing up subject responsibilities among the various committee members
>
> ensuring that members receive notice of recommended sources, as well as the chance to look over all items already received that are under consideration for reference, before any meetings where decisions are made
>
> providing a method for members to record their opinions on sources under consideration before the meeting and making these opinions available to all other members
>
> reserving discussions at meetings to items with which there is disagreement among committee members
>
> reserving discussions at meetings to items considered typically problematic due to format or cost

Committee of Reference and Other Librarians

Some libraries prefer to broaden their reference selection committees with members from other library departments. Frequently, this will include bibliographers and acquisitions staff. One benefit that can be gained from this model is the chance to bring various collection development and reference services perspectives together, with each group learning from the other; a more careful integration of collection development with public services may evolve as a result. The disadvantages of this model have previously been considered: committees naturally take longer to complete some of these tasks than do individuals, and it is possible for librarians from areas outside reference to push for the selection of products that reference staff would find less than useful. Perhaps the best solution to the latter problem is to appoint one of the reference librarians as the committee chair so that reference concerns can be kept in the proper priority.

Consortium Committees

The expense of library collections in general has forged agreements among libraries to share expenses by cooperatively purchasing certain resources. In the past, this has usually involved especially expensive print publications that were not expected to receive heavy use but were still deemed important enough to require some access. Therefore, one library would agree to purchase an expensive set and maintain it, while another library would agree to purchase a different title and make it available to the group. This was sometimes agreed to in formal contractual terms within the auspices of an explicit consortium of libraries, and at other times there has been an implicit verbal understanding among libraries. The agreements were also among libraries that usually were relatively close geographically so that users from one library could travel easily to another library to use a source. (Library systems or states with strong commitments to resource sharing, such as the University of California library system and the state of Illinois, have provided rapid delivery via courier services to expand the geographic limits of their consortia.)

These sort of consortial arrangements often have involved reference titles that were quite expensive and were used infrequently; common candidates have included specialized periodical indexing and abstracting services and retrospective bibliographies of national libraries or major research institutions. In the current era, however, consortial agreements are more likely to involve electronic versions of these same types of tools. Publishers and vendors of online bibliographic services have attempted to expand their share of the reference market by granting substantial price discounts to customers with more users. Thus libraries have found that they are able to save considerable sums of money by entering into a contract with other libraries for these services. In fact, due to the expense of some services, small libraries with small budgets have often found that consortial purchasing is the only way that they could afford to offer the services to their users.

Also changing is the need for libraries to be in some geographical proximity to create these consortial agreements. Although there are some definite advantages to providing electronic resources to a more closely spaced group of libraries—the likelihood of national Internet backbone services creating delivery problems is diminished, for example—there are any number of consortia with members located quite some distance apart. Trinity University, for instance, belongs to one consortium called the Associated Colleges of the South, which includes this south Texan university as well as the University of Richmond in Virginia. Some of the consortium's shared electronic resources are made available over the Internet from vendors in Michigan and Ohio, states in which no consortium members reside. The geographic separateness of the members did not have any real importance to the information providers with whom we discussed purchases.

The decision-making situation for a consortium that wants to purchase reference products is a bit more complicated than that of a single library. At the level of the consortium, the libraries need to decide whether they will approach electronic product vendors as a formal, legal entity that signs a contract as one organization or whether they will simply use the consortium as an informal means to round up a group of purchasers. Most vendors will favor the first alternative, since they will argue that they can offer potentially greater savings to a group that appears as one entity, requiring only one billing invoice and one contact point for the vendor. However, vendors have also been willing to offer a group discount based on the size of the consortium, and bill each library individually. More than likely, the ability to continue individual library billing will depend in part on how important a resource provider considers the acquisition of this particular consortium's account.

In terms of selecting the most appropriate reference sources for a consortium, the decisions on these products are usually made at a higher level than those for materials added to a single library. Very often a committee of library directors or chief collection development officers will meet to decide on this issue. If a consortium is sufficiently large—say, an entire state network—then probably only appointed or elected representatives from some of the consortium's member libraries will make up the selection committee. The process of selecting reference sources that are most appropriate for a local library is greatly compromised in this scenario; small libraries are less likely to have as much determination in this process as large libraries that serve many more users.

Within the more locally oriented consortia, processes can ensure a better match of reference sources with a library's needs. The most important obligation of the consortium's selection committee is to receive ample input from all member libraries. This means that reference librarians from each of the institutions must be willing to investigate the products under consideration and communicate their recommendations in a clear and forceful way. In the end, staff must be willing to accept the trade-offs that come from entering into any sort of cooperative agreement of this nature.

The Importance of Reference Collection Management

In the descriptions of various alignments of library staff for the selection of reference sources, there are several places where the selection process can be derailed—where sources that should be added to the collection are not and items that do not belong are included. The reasons mentioned for this arise sometimes from a mistaken view about who should be responsible for buying which items and sometimes merely from inattention to the collection. These problems indicate that a library cannot depend on just one or several librarians adding new materials to the collection as they see fit. What is needed is active *management* of the reference collection.

Oversight Responsibility

Managing the collection requires that some staff member or members be assigned oversight of the entire process to ensure the adequacy of the reference collection for current library needs. The person or persons charged with oversight can check to see that

> the appropriate sources have in fact been added to the collection
> useful interdisciplinary titles have not slipped through the cracks of a subject-discipline division of labor
> too much of the reference budget is not being spent on areas that receive limited amounts of use
> areas of the collection in need of weeding or updating are given attention

The way that this oversight is established in various libraries will vary, often according to the political climate in those libraries. It is possible to assign the oversight to a committee, as long as those committee members are given clearly defined objectives and tasks. However, cooperative management of the reference collection becomes more unwieldy than cooperative selection and weeding. Many of the daily activities involved in managing the reference collection require quick decisions on sources to add or delete from the collection, and this sort of activity can be cumbersome in a committee. Instead, most libraries will find it more efficient to assign the oversight of reference collection management to just one individual.

The staff member assigned to oversee the collection does not need to be the head of the reference department, although that position is one logical place to put the responsibility. It is quite feasible to assign this role to another reference librarian; in fact, many reference departments have one person serving as coordinator of their reference collections, another in charge of library instruction or online services, and so on. The chosen staff member must be able to maintain an overarching perspective on the success of the reference collection in meeting the needs of library users and reference staff.

What is required of the library's management, however, is that the person chosen to oversee the collection's management be given a clearly delineated area of responsibility and the clear authority to make the final decisions that must be made. Since there will be occasions when this person will need to overrule colleagues on their decisions to locate or remove an item from reference, clear lines of authority are necessary.

Intralibrary Cooperation

The appointment of a staff member to oversee all aspects of the reference collection will provide a good basis for maintaining its quality. However, the objective of creating an excellent reference collection cannot reside only with reference staff. Reference staff do not work alone in acquiring sources for the collection; several other library departments provide their input in this process. The technical services departments of a library, including cataloging and acquisitions, are important to the success of the reference collection. A good technical services staff will realize that they, too, are providing a public service in their roles in getting the appropriate sources into the hands of library users.

Reference staff need to have a good working relationship with these departments. Acquisitions staff must be kept aware of the importance of the reference sources to the services provided to users. This implies that reference sources are ordered as promptly as possible, problems with acquiring sources are communicated quickly back to the selector, and problems with critical reference serial subscriptions are resolved immediately.

Cataloging staff are central to the processing of new items for the reference collection and the relocation or withdrawal of outdated materials. Again, the importance of reference materials to the reference department's activities necessitates that new sources be promptly cataloged and made available. Many libraries will want to consider procedures that place reference materials high on the priority list of items to be processed. Reference staff also need to have a responsive cataloging department when they discover that particular forms of subject or other access through the library's catalog are not working well for their designed purposes. A good working relationship requires that each department attempt to view the problem through the eyes of public service needs as well as cataloging requirements for meeting standards. Finally, the weeding of reference collections is sometimes stymied by the low priority given it by very busy catalogers. Reference staff must be able to articulate the reasons why outdated reference sources lower the quality of the reference collection and should be removed promptly after the request for removal is given.

Notes

1. Rebecca Kroll, "The Place of Reference Collection Development in the Organizational Structure of the Library," *RQ* 25 (fall 1985): 96–7.

2. Kroll, "Place," p. 97.

3. Scott Stebelman, "The Role of Subject Specialists in Reference Collection Development," *RQ* 29 (winter 1989): 266–9.

4. Stebelman, "The Role of Subject Specialists," p. 271.

5. See some useful tips on handling this sort of position in "Guidelines for Liaison Work," *RQ* 32 (winter 1992): 198–204, as well as survey results in *Liaison Services in ARL Libraries,* SPEC Kit no. 199, comp. Gail F. Latta (Washington, D.C.: Association of Research Libraries, 1992).

6. Daniel T. Richards and Dottie Eakin, *Collection Development and Assessment in Health Science Libraries,* vol. 4 of *Current Practice in*

Health Sciences Librarianship, ed. Alison Bunting (Lanham, Md., and London: Medical Library Association and Scarecrow Press, 1997), p. 20.

7. Rebecca Schreiner-Robles and Malcolm Germann, "Workload of Reference-Bibliographers in Medium-Sized Academic Libraries," *RQ* 29 (fall 1989): 84–5.

8. Marcia J. Bates, "What Is a Reference Book? A Theoretical and Empirical Analysis," *RQ* 26 (fall 1986): 48–54.

∾ 4 ∾
Selection Principles

Establishing the types of materials that are desired in a reference collection and who will be responsible for selecting these sources are important steps to take before sources are purchased. With this grounding from a reference collection development policy, selectors may then begin to search for reference sources that are appropriate for the local collection. (If the library has a collection role in a consortium, that must be considered as well.) The next step is finding a way to identify materials that are candidates for selection. The final section of this chapter discusses published sources that provide lists of titles and evaluative information about them. Before beginning to read publishers' brochures or professional reviews, however, it is helpful to know what elements make a reference source a good acquisition. Even with the help of professional reviewers, a reference selector must ultimately make an individual determination about a prospective reference source's value for his or her own collection.

General Selection Criteria

In chapter 1 several important criteria for adding an information source to the reference collection were given:

- arranged in a reference format: designed for quick consultation
- frequently used: consisting of useful tools, not deadwood
- authoritative: accurate and reliable
- current
- unique coverage: providing some form of information or access that other sources have not provided

These criteria do not begin to exhaust the qualities that differentiate the best reference sources from those that are mediocre or even badly done. Lists of evaluative criteria have been proposed by quite a number of authors; beginning reference textbooks nearly always contain them.[1] There is a great deal of overlap among these various lists. All of these criteria are worthy of consideration, but the distinctions are sometimes drawn too finely. As Stevens points out, there are theoretical review criteria, and then there are practical criteria that often carry the most importance with selectors.[2] Few selectors can spend substantial time evaluating one source on a wide variety of detailed points unless the high cost of that source makes the decision especially worrisome. What follows is a list of criteria that appear most valuable for normal selection, once the basic characteristics previously listed have been met. Note that some of these characteristics are interrelated, and it is difficult to consider one of them totally on its own. Additionally, some of the basic criteria can be addressed fully only when the other characteristics have also been evaluated.

Also note that all of these criteria can—and should—be applied to electronic sources as well as traditional printed reference books. (They may also be applied to the small number of reference sources that are published in microform or in other nonprint media.) Certainly, there are some differences that must be considered when looking at materials in different media; for example, paper and binding quality can matter for a book, while the preservation issues for a CD-ROM or an Internet-based subscription are different. The next chapter, dealing with electronic reference tools, addresses many of the specific concerns of that medium. However, the basic principles for evaluating the quality and usefulness of the source do not vary among the different formats.

The major selection criteria include

- scope
- comprehensiveness
- audience
- documentation
- design
- indexing
- bibliography
- illustrations
- durability
- format
- cost

Scope

What subjects does a reference source attempt to cover? The author or editor of a work must have carefully delineated the source's scope during its execution if that source is to do its job well. Users need to know what a source purports to cover to decide whether it is a tool they can turn to for their queries. Reference selectors prefer an explicit statement of scope to evaluate the source's coverage. The best reference sources will describe exactly what subjects they attempted to cover in the work and which related subjects were omitted. Printed reference sources usually include a scope note in the preface or introduction to the work; electronic databases may include it on a greeting screen, in the help system, or in the accompanying manual. Unfortunately, more than a few sources omit any detailed description of their scope, and the selector must attempt to guess this from a perusal of the work.

The scope note will include different information depending on the type of reference source. Always helpful are comments about any limits on the coverage of the subjects; at what date no further information was added to the work (for example, the cutoff date after which no new bibliographic entries were gathered); and whether information from various countries and in various languages was considered, or if the work is limited to sources from just one of these. Selectors will also find it quite helpful if the author has described how the work compares with others already available. Is the work more current, more comprehensive, or arranged in a new way that facilitates its use? Of course, the selector must verify that the author's claims in this regard are true, but there is substantial benefit from reading what the author believes the uniqueness of the work to be.

Prospective purchasers of a reference work should also note that the scope of the work directly affects its likelihood of being used. More than a few reference publishers have been creating new works that cover smaller and smaller areas of information. These restricted-scope works may be useful in a few libraries, but many libraries have little need for these items. It is doubtful, for example, that most reference collections would profit from adding books that merely list the titles and basic plots (such as they are) of a few years' episodes from television sitcoms—yet these types of books are produced and acquired.

Comprehensiveness

Once the subject matter of the work is determined, the selector must evaluate the depth with which the particular subject is covered. For a bibliography, for example, does the work cover everything published about a subject during a certain period, or is some selectivity being used? A good reference work need not be totally comprehensive within its scope; a thoughtfully annotated bibliography of works that the author considers most important can often be more useful than an exhaustive listing of every published work. Many academic librarians find that beginning undergraduates can be overwhelmed by the comprehensiveness of the *MLA International Bibliography* or *PsycINFO*, and briefer bibliographic tools may be easier to use. Librarians may wish to purchase sources that primarily index what is in their own collections, so the most comprehensive tools may not be as attractive to them. Yet there are many occasions when a library user wants to find everything possible about a particular subject, and shallow coverage in a bibliographic source will be unsuitable.

Periodical indexes and certain other bibliographic resources can be judged on their comprehensiveness more easily than other sources because they usually list the primary materials that they index. Users can have a more difficult time trying to evaluate the coverage of other reference tools, such as biographical dictionaries or subject encyclopedias. In these types of tools, shallowness of coverage can be discovered only through many attempts to locate specific information by a reviewer who knows what should be included in the source. Unless the reference sources are oriented to a very general audience, and this audience is important to the library's mission, works that cover their subjects in a cursory manner are usually poor additions to the reference collection.

Audience

The level at which a reference source is written affects its ease of use by different library users. The author's determination of intended audience will be reflected in the choice of subject, of course, but also in the depth of coverage given to the subject and the sophistication of the author's writing. Sources created for use by children will naturally tend to have less detail and simpler prose than those intended for adult readers. Those sources aimed at professionals in a discipline will usually have much greater depth of coverage and will be written with greater use of technical jargon (and, all too often, greater use of stultifying academic prose). Reference selectors find it useful to match up sources designed for particular audiences with the library clientele that fit these descriptions. This is more difficult than it seems, for many libraries serve a wide range of users who have varying levels of intellectual development. Thus many libraries will want to have reference sources covering the same subjects but aimed at different audiences, whether they be as distinct as adults and young children or closer in level, as undergraduates are to professors. Naturally, the library will be purchasing some sources that appear to duplicate each other but that will actually be used by very different segments of their user populations.

Reference librarians should not assume that reference tools written with beginning or less-sophisticated learners in mind are useful only for children. Our society is full of adults who are learning a second language or are marginally literate and could be served well by sources usually considered children's reference tools; these titles can be quite valuable in public libraries (though shelving them all in a separate children's reference collection might discourage adult use). Also to be heeded is the nature of the reference collection as a starting point for users of the library. Those who are beginning to research a topic quite new to them are not served well by the presence of only sophisticated sources in reference. Even those people who are quite adept with the literature in one field may have use for a simplified encyclopedia covering an unfamiliar discipline. The *World Book Encyclopedia,* for instance, supposedly aimed at the children's market, is quite popular with and works nicely for adults, who enjoy the clear language and arrangement.

Documentation

A reference source should be authoritative, meaning that its accuracy and reliability are not typically questioned. This sort of authority is usually earned after repeated use and the determination by users of the source's dependability. However, any source should be able to stand up to questioning about the origin of its facts. A good reference source will document the sources that were used in its compilation and usually give enough information to permit a user to backtrack and ascertain the correctness of the reference tool's statements. For encyclopedias, almanacs, handbooks, and biographical and statistical sources, each article or table should have some indication of the source of the information, most often coming in one or more citations to other sources. Atlases that contain topical maps based on demographic or weather data, for example, should also provide citations to the source of the data.

Documentation is a different issue for sources like dictionaries, bibliographies, and indexes. General dictionaries, with the exception of massive works like the *Oxford English Dictionary*, do not cite the history of each word they define; instead, they describe the process of compiling the definitions in a preface. Bibliographic sources point directly to the citations themselves, which can easily be verified, but good bibliographies and periodical indexes will carefully indicate what other sources were consulted in compiling the works.

Documenting the information in a reference source also includes the identification of the author or compiler of the information. In sources that provide other forms of documentation, the authority of the author adds to the user's estimations of the information's worthiness. In sources that provide no other documentation, the author's and publisher's reputations may be the only ways to gauge the trust that one can place in the sources (at least until a more thorough review and fact-checking process can take place). Thus a work like a subject encyclopedia that fails to attribute the authorship of its articles is cause for concern. Many sources attempt to minimize individual authorship statements within the body of the works, often using the authors' initials instead of their full names at the end of articles. Yet those who wish to check on the authors' credentials can find a list of these experts elsewhere within the source.

Design

Design is also sometimes referred to as "arrangement" or "interface," the latter being used especially for electronic products. The design of a reference source determines how well users are directed to the information they are trying to find. Design includes the physical arrangement of the parts of a reference tool.

> Do the sections fit together and flow logically from one section to another?
>
> Is it easy to understand what data are being presented and where they are located?
>
> Does the arrangement of material suit the subject of the work?

For example, many monographic subject bibliographies order their citations in alphabetical order by author. When considering that users turn to these reference books to find materials on a subject, not to locate a known author, the arrangement seems to be virtually irrelevant to the source's function. Unless the bibliography has an excellent index or provides at least some subject classification, its usefulness in a reference collection is suspect.

Also included in design are characteristics such as legibility and the ability to browse easily. Poorly constructed tables of data (perhaps from inferior camera-ready copy) or maps on which labels cannot be accurately read are examples of poor design that hinder the functionality of the sources. Browsability is an important result of good design that permits users to move among the various sections of a work without losing track of where they are. The use of clear headers on all pages, differences in typefaces to indicate different elements in the information records, and descriptive information at the point of need (such as the repetition of major abbreviations at the bottom of each dictionary page) all can make a source much easier for an inexperienced user to browse.

For electronic reference products, design elements determine how easy it is to use the search software, how uncluttered screen displays are, and other characteristics of the user-machine interface. Some differences between electronic and printed sources in this area

are discussed in the next chapter. However, many of the same principles of good design for print products also apply to computer-based
sources: clarity of display, methods to keep one's place in the system,
and logical flow from one part of the system to another.

According to Lang, design may also be thought of as including an
evaluation of the literary or artistic merits of a publication.[3] The reference source that users remember for its artistry is infrequent, but
some reference tools present their information so elegantly that users
become particularly fond of them. Although reference librarians no
doubt wish that all library users (and maybe all librarians) would read
the prefatory material to a reference book, very few do so. The well-
designed reference source, which might be considered to exhibit artistic or literary excellence, is often fully understandable without reading
any of the accompanying preface or explanations.

Indexing

The existence of a good index to a reference publication is so obvious
that it is almost taken for granted. An index to a reference book provides additional methods of accessing the information in the work.
Even the best-designed printed source is limited by the two-
dimensional nature of the printed page; it is not feasible to arrange the
information in every possible permutation that a user might need. Indexes provide a way to hunt down those other occurrences of a topic
that the user did not find under the compiler's headings. Simpler indexes have one point of access: the single topic or name with its list of
appearances in the volume. More complex indexes list many of the
topics as subdivisions under other subjects, effectively correlating two
or more concepts in the same index entries. In spite of their obvious
utility, indexes are often cursory efforts or are even occasionally omitted. In these cases, the main body of the work must be designed extremely well to make up for the omission.

Indexing is not just a feature at the end of a book. Another type of
indexing is the use of cross references, notations within the main sections of the source that point the reader to another place in the source.
Cross references are needed for two main purposes. First, users are always confronted by the problem of vocabulary: the word that one person might use to describe a concept is not the same as another person's
word. Recognizing this fact, reference source authors will insert refer-

ences from a term not used as an entry to the term that they did choose. For example, an American history encyclopedia may have a cross reference from the topic "American Revolution," under which there is no article, to the place where this topic is discussed under the term, "War of Independence." Second, cross references can point a user to related entries that are not covered in the present entry, thus providing additional avenues for finding information.

Cross references are especially plentiful in high-quality encyclopedias, dictionaries, library catalogs, periodical indexes, and bibliographies. Electronic sources sometimes dispense with cross references in the belief that the ability to search by keyword will offset any need for them. Indeed, keyword searching can provide sophisticated access to reference works, offering the user a multitude of possibilities for combining different concepts. However, the existence of human-created cross references continues to serve as an important supplement to machine indexing. The best electronic periodical indexes and abstracts are usually based on a subject thesaurus, which provides a cross-reference structure to the database. Well-designed products take advantage of this structure by permitting users to redirect searches from unused terms to the authorized vocabulary. Additionally, the current developments in hypertext provide another option for cross-referencing, permitting the user to move to related entries from within the current document. *Britannica Online,* the online counterpart of the printed *Encyclopaedia Britannica,* offers these sorts of links within many of its articles. Users can read an article, explore an embedded concept that needs clarification by the use of a cross-reference link (or "hyperlink"), and return easily to the original article. Virtually all reference sources should incorporate some degree of cross-referencing in their design.

Bibliography

A set of bibliographic citations accompanying an entry in a reference source can serve as documentation of its reliability. However, a bibliography also provides more than just support for the reference work. Users come to the reference section in part to find answers quickly. They also come looking for a place to start when confronted with a large library collection. When they turn to an encyclopedia, a handbook, or another reference source, they hope to find some of the information for which they are searching. Additionally, users are directed to other sources through the bibliographies that should be present in these types of tools.

Lists of sources for further reading need not be extensive in many reference sources. Perhaps more useful is the list that contains carefully chosen sources that are helpful for the novice in that subject area. Those persons with a substantial knowledge of a discipline are less likely to need a subject encyclopedia, for example; the bibliographies in these works should be oriented toward the less knowledgeable reader. Especially useful are lists of classic and "must-know" sources that could bring a less informed person up to speed on that subject. The exception to this may be a specialized subject handbook, which is likely to have more appeal to professionals in the fields covered and which may serve its users better with more-sophisticated suggested readings.

Illustrations

Many reference works are primarily textual, containing little in the way of illustrative matter. For some sources, this is not a concern; the *Statistical Abstract of the United States* and the *National Union Catalog* have served well without the use of pictures. However, a good number of reference sources profit considerably from the inclusion of illustrations. It could be argued that library users are increasingly expecting to find information in graphical form, considering the developments of newspaper graphics, cable television, videotapes, and multimedia computer applications (including the World Wide Web). Many reference publishers have followed this trend. Multimedia encyclopedias on CD-ROM are quite common, and printed encyclopedias have also included more illustrations. The *Academic American Encyclopedia* is profusely illustrated in color, as is the *World Book Encyclopedia,* and even the traditional *Collier's Encyclopedia* has felt the need to advertise about its increased use of graphics.

Care should be taken to give illustrations the appropriate amount of credit for enhancing the usefulness of a reference work. In encyclopedias and biographical sources, photographs and drawings can provide a fine way to clarify the subject discussed in the accompanying prose. Illustrations need not be high-resolution color photographs; the *McGraw-Hill Encyclopedia of Science and Technology* does an excellent job with many simple, two-color drawings. However, quite a few smaller subject encyclopedias offer poorly reproduced graphics, apparently in the hope of making the work more salable. Instead, they do little but add to the cost of the material.

Unfortunately, cost is one of the trade-offs of including illustrations in a reference work. Attractive full-color photographs will significantly increase a book's price. Selectors need to analyze whether an expensive source is worth the higher price dictated by the use of illustrations. Storage space and speed of access are other trade-offs when electronic reference sources are reviewed. Their high-resolution illustrations create greatly increased file sizes compared with text-only entries. Most CD-ROM versions of large reference works, like *Encyclopaedia Britannica,* have included only some of the graphics from the printed work, and online versions available through the Internet have had minimal graphics up to this point. (There is a move to increase the use of graphics in these sources.) In certain subjects, reference works cannot do their job well without illustrations—consider an art encyclopedia. However, many sources still function well without graphics, so the reference selector should consider the presence or absence of illustrations according to the benefit derived in that particular subject and genre of reference tool.

Durability

If reference sources have been chosen carefully for the collection, they should receive at least a fair amount of use from library patrons and librarians. Thus the materials should survive this level of use. For printed sources, the selector should be concerned with the paper quality (acid-free should be mandatory) and the sturdiness of the binding. Most reference sources still receive a hard cover, which protects the work to some degree, but spiraling costs are increasing the number of paperbacks entering reference collections. In terms of durability, the issue of hardcover versus paperbacks is mostly a decision related to the permanence desired for the work.

Of special concern is the way the pages are sewn into the binding. Reference sources are frequently opened to a page while a user hand copies information, so the ability of the book to open as flat as possible and stay open is important. The ubiquitous use of photocopies, with the scenario of books being pressed down hard on the glass of the copiers, also requires that these books open flat without damage to the binding. Those that are likely to be copied regularly should also have sufficiently large gutter margins, so that users are not encouraged to press down hard just to copy the area near the binding. Sources that fail this test and are heavily used are very likely to lose their pages.

Some sources, however, may be considered only temporary acquisitions, soon to be replaced with updated versions. *Value Line,* for instance, is a loose-leaf serial that is printed on newsprint. The archival qualities of this tool are nil, but the source serves mainly as a current-awareness tool for investors. Thus there is little need for great expense in the paper and binding of this type of work.

Durability is also an issue to consider with some electronic sources. CD-ROM tools, for instance, seem impervious to the types of damage mentioned for books. Yet these discs can be dropped, inserted into the wrong drive on a computer, warped by the heat of a car's dashboard, or otherwise rendered unplayable. Reference sources that come on diskettes have similar potential dangers. These risks to their permanence are not individualistic to different reference sources; they are characteristics of everything in those media. Selectors should not ignore the issue of durability or permanence, however, especially if a library's only copy of that data is on one disc or diskette. Librarians should ask themselves what their options will be if the media itself becomes unusable. Can the publisher supply another copy of the disc (and if so, at what cost), or are the data available in another form?

Format

There is nothing intrinsically superior overall of one format over others, but selectors should evaluate how well the format of a reference source fits the way a library's users need to get their information. Print has a long and successful history of supplying information to readers, and nothing about current technological developments has diminished its qualities. The superior readability, the easy ability to browse and keep track of one's place, and the lack of reliance on the newest computer hardware or the speed of the Internet make printed reference tools quite sufficient for many applications.

Microforms are probably becoming an even smaller part of most reference collections than they were in the past, as loading the same data onto CD-ROM discs is frequently as easy and relatively inexpensive. Microforms have probably never been a favorite format for library users, so the selection of tools in microfiche or microfilm should be limited to those few sources that work well in this medium. Directories, simple dictionary catalogs, and reproductions of lengthy printed works that do not require extensive amounts of reading (such as college catalogs and some government documents) are suited to microform. Besides the obvious advantage in saving valuable shelf space, microforms are also a proven medium for archiving data. Unlike compact discs, for which there are still questions about longevity, microfilm and microfiche can last many decades with little degradation. However, patrons often complain about being required to use microforms, and complaints also come from library staff who are faced with the difficulty of keeping large microfiche sets in proper filing order.

Reference works in audiovisual format are not particularly common in most libraries. Most reference departments are not equipped to handle the playing of videorecordings, cassette tapes, films, slides, and so on. Many of the traditional audiovisual formats are also not conducive to quick consultation, due to the lack of random-access movement on tapes and films. It is feasible that special library reference collections, such as in an art library or a music library, could profitably place slide sets or digital recordings into a reference collection. Also, many medical libraries may put videotapes into a reference collection for in-house use, but this designation is usually not much more than a substitute for reserve or noncirculating status. We are likely to see the development of more sophisticated multimedia applications in the future, however, and many of these will provide the quick access to specific information required of reference materials.

Digital multimedia products are merely the latest in the great increase in electronic products that reference collections consider acquiring. Electronic sources bring definite advantages and disadvantages as a format, which will be considered in detail in the next chapter. It is sufficient to mention for now that librarians are being faced with pressure to buy reference tools in electronic form in addition to or in place of printed sources, and the electronic products are among the most popular sources in today's reference collections.

Cost

Cost is the last criterion in this list not because it is the least important, but because the final decision on adding or not adding a source often must be based on an evaluation of its cost. The cost of a reference source can be considered in both an absolute and a relative framework. The absolute cost of a source is simply the actual price that a library must pay for it. A dictionary that costs $195 will remove just that amount from the library's budget. This cost can easily be compared with the cost of competing sources.

However, the absolute cost of a source does not necessarily determine whether it is a better selection than another source. A selector must judge the value of one source's information per cost unit against that of another source. That is, a more expensive source may do a much better job of covering the subject for which it was published than a less expensive source does. The utility of the expensive source may cause it to be used more and provide better service to the library's users, avoiding the waste of staff time when they must use inferior sources, and perhaps avoiding the need to purchase other materials on this subject. Therefore, its relative cost may be lower than the cheaper source.

Of course, no selector purchases library materials without consideration of the library's budget. This is another point at which costs are relative, in this case to each library's financial situation. The fixed annual budget for a reference department collection requires that choices be made according to the maximum benefit that can be derived from those funds. Therefore, a selector may be forced to buy somewhat lower quality reference sources to save money for other purchases. The new $3,000 subject encyclopedia in physiology may be an essential purchase for a medical library with a large budget, but it might be out of the question for a hospital library with a much smaller budget. Thus the reference selector must constantly evaluate the value of a source against its price, keeping in mind other items that will need to be acquired during the rest of the budget cycle.

Source-Specific Selection Criteria

Many authors, notably those of library science textbooks, have discussed the features of various types of reference sources in considerable detail, demonstrating how to thoroughly evaluate them.[4] These same textbooks list many examples for each category of reference tool, but the lists tend to become dated, and they will not be duplicated here. However, some additional evaluative factors are pertinent to particular types of tools, which can be helpful to the typical selector who has too few funds for too many potential reference titles.

General Encyclopedias

Encyclopedias are, of course, among the most basic sources in any reference collection and deserve some extended consideration. A general encyclopedia is a compendium of the world's knowledge, providing basic information on just about any subject. While a large variety of specialized encyclopedias have been and continue to be published, the number of general, broad-coverage sets is relatively small. (This no doubt results from the significant costs and efforts required to produce an entirely new encyclopedia as well as the dominant market position held by the publishers of several worthy sets.) Most libraries of any size whatsoever usually own more than one of these major sets because even the relative comprehensiveness of the sets does not avoid differences in coverage and treatment of topics. Due to the expense of the large general encyclopedias and the fact that most have only small amounts of their texts revised in any one year, many libraries have typically purchased several titles on a rotating basis, buying one title one year, another the next, and perhaps a third or fourth in the following years. This allows the collection to have at least one very recent edition while still providing access to alternate points of view.

Because of the stability of the publishing situation with general encyclopedias, the reference selector has little trouble determining the top titles from which to choose—in the world of print. Among English-language encyclopedias, the *New Encyclopaedia Britannica, Encyclopedia Americana*, and *Collier's Encyclopedia* are well-established as the leaders in both quantity and quality of coverage. It is not at all uncommon to find all three sets in the collections of large public and academic libraries in this country. Yes, there are differences among them, and those who wish can find very good reviews in the professional literature.[5] Most reviewers would agree that all are fine choices. Likewise, similar opinions can be found for the major children's encyclopedias in print today.

The complications that arise in the selection of encyclopedias today come from the emergence of electronic versions of these three and several other sources. All three of the big general titles, plus several other smaller sets, are currently available on CD-ROM. Many of the encyclopedias have been available in one form or another online as well. For instance, *Britannica* and *Americana* have Internet sites that allow subscribers to connect using Web browser software on their computer workstations. Several encyclopedias have had their text available through proprietary online services, such as America Online and CompuServe. To further complicate matters, various combinations of print, CD-ROM, and online access are available. For example, purchasers of Microsoft's *Encarta* CD-ROM encyclopedia (based largely on the print *Funk & Wagnall's New Encyclopedia*) are authorized to connect to Microsoft's Internet site to access and download revisions and additions to the CD-ROM's content.

The emergence of the CD-ROM encyclopedia has particularly been a major boon for home users. Although many people have wanted to own a current encyclopedia in their homes, costs of the major print sets are quite high (near or more than $1,000), they take up quite a bit of physical space, and much of their content becomes dated. As of early 1998, careful shoppers were able to purchase multimedia CD-ROM versions of the big three encyclopedias for less than $100 each. Other encyclopedias such as *Encarta* have routinely sold for less than $50. Given this very affordable price range, the lack of required shelf space, and the benefits of online updating or the affordability of buying a new edition, the comprehensive encyclopedia has become an easy acquisition for homes with personal computers.

Libraries are faced with more difficult decisions, however. Standalone CD-ROM versions have been selected in many libraries, especially small libraries, but there is some loss for the many gains of the electronic versions. Printed encyclopedias typically allow more than one user, as long as the additional users want to use different volumes than the other users do. For libraries to provide this multiuser capability with compact disc versions, they must network the CD-ROM or purchase several copies. However, as prices for the CD versions continue to plunge, the purchase of multiple copies or multiple titles on CD has become much more feasible for even small libraries. Of course, as discussed in further detail in the next chapter, selectors must consider the issue of having enough computer workstations for the products (and the costs of purchasing and maintaining this equipment).

To provide remote access to an electronic encyclopedia, many libraries in the past loaded the text of an encyclopedia onto their library system hardware. Although this may have provided a relatively easy way to share the data, networking costs were often significant, and the information was often limited to text without any graphics. Furthermore, libraries usually loaded only a single encyclopedia in this manner, which failed to give users the benefits of comparing several of the major titles. This mode of remote access is rapidly being replaced with access through the World Wide Web in libraries with Internet connections. *Britannica* and *Americana* both offer access to their full text plus many graphics through the Web, and these versions also include links to pertinent Internet sites and additional articles not found in the print version. Web access provides probably the easiest installation of all the networked or remote-access methods because the data are kept at the publishers' Web sites and users need only use any of the common Web browsers as an interface.

How does a reference selector choose from among the many options for these titles? A selector can look at four principal niches to fill with encyclopedias, depending on the funding available and the users that a library wants to serve:

1. *Comprehensive Printed Encyclopedias*   In spite of the use of electronic versions, there is little evidence that users will stop using printed encyclopedias; instead, there is increased use of the printed versions once electronic versions are made available.[6] Most libraries will still want to own one or more of the big three sets for their ease of use, quick referral, dependability without computer aid, and archival qualities. (The permanence of the printed version should not be underestimated, for the ongoing revision of the online editions leads to the "disappearance" of what was written in earlier editions. Users cannot compare the treatment of a subject over time when only the online version is available.)

2. *Electronic Encyclopedias*   The capabilities of keyword searching, hyperlinks to cross-references, more-frequent revisions, and remote access possibilities make CD-ROM or Web-based encyclopedias a must purchase for almost every library. Those libraries with smaller budgets may be able to offer the same number of comprehensive titles formerly provided only by much larger libraries. Although some of the less-expensive CD-ROM encyclopedias have attractive graphics, the new pricing structure of the major sets makes the smaller competitors distinctly secondary purchases for most libraries, except for the titles oriented to children.

3. *Less Comprehensive Printed Encyclopedias* In today's world of television and other graphical media, many users seem more interested in using sources that have more appeal than the largely textual comprehensive sets. Titles such as the *Academic American Encyclopedia, Compton's Encyclopedia,* and even the *World Book Encyclopedia* may appeal to both adults and younger readers by virtue of their somewhat shorter articles and heavy use of illustrations. Consider these titles in addition to the three comprehensive sets, not in place of them, in any reference collection other than one exclusively for young children.

4. *Children's Encyclopedias* These sets are necessary both for children who are not able to comprehend the text in adult-oriented titles and those adults whose reading skills are minimal. While some younger readers will be able to use *Britannica* or *Collier's,* most libraries will need to provide other sets appropriate for the youngest readers, such as *The New Book of Knowledge,* and titles geared to other youth, such as the aforementioned *World Book, Compton's,* or *The New Standard Encyclopedia.*

Many of the encyclopedias have traditionally updated their information continuously, meaning that some proportion of the entire work is revised for each year's edition. To supplement the existing editions already purchased, publishers have produced yearbooks. The yearbooks do not actually update many of the specific articles of the parent set; instead, they attempt to capture the major events and discoveries of the year in one volume. Are these essential purchases for reference collections? In most cases, yearbooks tend to receive little use by the public and may be optional purchases. The strongest benefit of a yearbook is that it can be useful for a student or researcher who wants to read contemporary writers' comments on a particular year's events. As a record of changing interpretation, it is a nice supplement to the main set. Note that it may be possible to have access to these yearbooks as part of an online subscription. *Britannica Online* currently does this for its subscribers, and the CD-ROM *Encarta* permits purchasers of certain versions to download updated articles and yearbook entries from its Web site.

What about the smaller, general encyclopedias that often are published in one volume? Examples of these include *The New Columbia Encyclopedia* and *The Cambridge Encyclopedia.* These sources are somewhat of a hybrid between multivolume encyclopedias and dictionaries. Articles are much shorter than those in the more comprehensive encyclopedias; therefore, one-volume sources of this type are useful for only the most basic ready-reference type of query. Users who are attempting to educate themselves on a particular subject will find the more comprehensive titles much more helpful. Although the good one-volume works are accurate and authoritative, their brevity suits them better for home use or for very small libraries that cannot afford the larger sets. The only significant usefulness for these titles may be placing them in the stacks of large libraries or in small branch libraries that have minimal general reference collections—places in which a large set is unavailable. In this case, the one-volume encyclopedia can supplement the dictionaries that are also frequently distributed throughout large libraries. However, if a networked or Web-based encyclopedia is readily available, along with distributed workstations, even this function may no longer be needed. Reference funds may be more profitably spent on other titles in most libraries.

Subject Encyclopedias

Unlike the general encyclopedias just described, subject encyclopedias are based on a subset of the world's knowledge and attempt to cover a significant portion of that subset. The scope of these works varies tremendously, as does the treatment. Some, such as *The McGraw-Hill Encyclopedia of Science and Technology* and the *International Encyclopedia of the Social Sciences,* have impressively large scopes, numbers of articles, and price tags. Other titles may be as specific as the *Encyclopedia of German Resistance to the Nazi Movement* and *The Blackwell Encyclopedia of Writing Systems.* Especially in academic libraries, these subject encyclopedias can be some of the most useful sources in the reference collection. They provide greater topic depth than most general encyclopedias and dictionaries, yet they still offer an understandable introduction to the topic and related subjects for the reader with little knowledge in that area.

There are a great many more subject encyclopedias than general ones; Kister's guide, for example, lists more than 800 current titles worthy of consideration.[7] The library catalog at Trinity University in early 1998 listed nearly 2,000 separate works as having the keywords "encyclopedia" or "encyclopedias" in their bibliographic records; UCLA's catalog listed more than 3,000 titles with "encyclopedias" in just the subject fields of their records. Of course, many of these titles use the word "encyclopedia" in their titles when, in fact, they are much closer to dictionaries in their treatment of the entries. However, this does not diminish the likelihood that a selector for the reference collection will encounter a large number of titles deserving some consideration, and some guidelines beyond the earlier-discussed criteria might be helpful.

Over the past couple of decades, reference publishers have noted library selectors' penchant to purchase subject encyclopedias, perhaps to the point that almost any subject encyclopedia is expected to sell well to libraries. As a result, many titles have been published that are either exceptionally narrow in scope or superficial in coverage. The latter type of source is easily determined to be unsuitable for purchase, but the narrow-scope work may well be a strong addition to its subject field. The selector should keep in mind the expectations of a new title's use when locating it in reference. Many of these subject sources with narrowly focused topics may be worthy additions to the main library collection but perhaps poorly suited for the reference collection. They would likely receive limited use by patrons, and these small-niche publications are also less likely to be remembered by the reference staff.

Also valuable in subject encyclopedias is the presence of reasonable length entries. In contrast, a number of encyclopedias have taken the approach of commissioning quite lengthy articles and providing few or no brief entries; recent examples include the *Encyclopedia of the American Judicial System* and *Civilizations of the Ancient Near East.* While these types of tools can be worthy sources (both of these were award-winning titles), the lengthiness of the entries makes it much more difficult to quickly locate a desired bit of information. Good indexes can help the user of these works, and *Civilizations of the Ancient Near East* has an excellent index of nearly 150 pages. However, the long essay format somewhat diminishes the encyclopedia's usefulness for ready reference queries, and anecdotal evidence suggests that these types of subject encyclopedias may receive less-frequent use than competing works that break up their texts into shorter entries. (Some works, of course, offer both major essays on broad topics and many briefer entries.)

Dictionaries

Dictionaries are another mainstay of every reference collection, offering brief to moderate-length definitions and explanations of various concepts. Many different types of dictionaries have been published, including unabridged and brief language dictionaries, subject dictionaries that cover the terms of a particular discipline, slang dictionaries, thesauri, and so on. The basic criteria of evaluating reference sources are also pertinent here. Accuracy and comprehensiveness are important, since dictionary users by intent are looking for quick, succinct answers to their questions and are not usually looking for a variety of sources to compare with each other. Currency can also be essential, as languages change and add new words or new meanings to old words. The major competing sources, at least in language dictionaries, are often quite similar in scope and content; therefore, special attention should be paid to features that distinguish one source from another. Especially useful in most dictionaries are definitions that include examples and illustrations. Both of these features can augment a textual definition that may not fully answer the user's questions. Also useful in large dictionaries with many abbreviations and symbols in their entries are legends appearing on every page or two, permitting the user to decipher the entries without constantly flipping back to a list of abbreviations in another location.

Library users frequently look for information on a particular topic and are pleased to find useful information under a number of related headings. However, dictionary users are frequently looking for the definition, pronunciation, etymology, or translation of specific words; related terms may not be of interest. Therefore, overlap among various sources can be desirable for dictionary collections because some sources will no doubt include different terms or definitions than other sources. Also, people will usually prefer to use a dictionary quickly while doing other reading or studying. Having multiple copies of popular dictionaries and placing them in several locations in a library, such as on dictionary stands on various floors, can allow their use with a minimum amount of disruption to the user.

Most libraries will want to own one or more unabridged dictionaries for the primary language of their users. In English, there are only a few titles that attempt to be comprehensive, and two of them are preeminent in the field: *Webster's Third New International Dictionary of the English Language, Unabridged,* and *The Random House Dictionary of the English Language.* Most libraries should own both. Due to their size, these titles are not easily portable. They are also updated infrequently and thus do not include the newest terms.

Supplements are available, but many users will find that newer editions of the abridged desk dictionaries do a fine job of keeping up with recent changes to the language. Thus, a wide selection of smaller, abridged language dictionaries that can be taken by users to their work area in the library can be quite useful and inexpensive. Of course, public and school libraries that support children's collections will need to purchase more-suitable titles for younger readers.

Dictionaries of foreign languages, including dual-language works that aid in translating, are staples for most reference collections. Again, this is an area where some duplication of sources is desirable because those who are translating may want to compare the translated definitions from more than one source. However, many reference collections contain an oversupply of foreign language dictionaries. Large research libraries, which support research in a wide range of languages, have reason to acquire dictionaries in many languages and to house them in their reference collections. Most libraries, though, can reasonably expect to need only a few dictionaries of other languages and can concentrate on placing these in reference. Other language dictionaries may indeed be purchased, but for only the very sporadic query, they may safely be shelved in the regular stacks.

Subject or technical dictionaries fill needs much like subject encyclopedias do: they provide understandable definitions in one or several related disciplines in a depth much greater than can be found in standard language dictionaries. Consequently, the most important consideration for technical dictionaries is whether they provide definitions that are clear to the user who is not a specialist in that subject area. Additionally, subject dictionaries that cover scientific areas, and especially medicine, must keep up with the rapid developments in those fields. Reference selectors must make sure that titles in these areas are up-to-date and include recent advances.

Bibliographies

There are many forms of bibliographic sources that libraries should consider selecting. Other than periodical indexes and abstracts, the major categories include national bibliographies, library catalogs, and subject bibliographies. National bibliographies include sources that are quite comprehensive in covering the publications originating in one country or in one language—such as the *British National Bibliog-*

raphy—and those—such as the *National Union Catalog (NUC)*—that cover holdings of a national library. The most comprehensive retrospective publication of this kind in the United States, which is still used frequently in many libraries, is the *National Union Catalog, Pre-1956 Imprints.* This massive 754-volume set provides bibliographic data on millions of titles and identifies more than 700 libraries owning these works. Subsequent versions of the *NUC* have provided updated lists of titles received by the Library of Congress and many libraries around the country for later years. The *NUC Pre-1956* and its successors have been essential sources for reference and interlibrary loan verification and for the location of libraries with copies of the desired titles.

However, in recent years the rise of national bibliographic utilities, or shared cataloging networks, has radically changed the nature of bibliographic work. OCLC and RLIN (the Research Libraries Information Network) are the two largest of these systems, providing access to tens of millions of bibliographic records for books, serials, and nonprint media. There are slight differences in the coverage of the two networks, as RLIN reflects principally the holdings of its 100 to 200 member research libraries, whereas OCLC contains contributed cataloging information from several thousand libraries, including the full gamut of libraries from small public and special libraries to large research institutions. Regardless of which network is used, reference librarians and users have sophisticated access by keyword, subject heading, media type, series title, and so on to these millions of records. As libraries have converted their catalogs into machine-readable form and retrospectively cataloged their older holdings, many of them have supplied this data to the shared databases. Thus the retrospective holdings of the databases have grown considerably, and many queries that would have involved using the *NUC* or another national bibliography are now solved easily with OCLC or RLIN. As of 1990 the *NUC* has stopped including items already loaded into these national databases.[8] However, note that not everything in the older *NUC* volumes has been added to these databases; consequently, the *NUC* still provides identification and verification services when searches in the online networks come up empty.

Less than ten years ago, it was uncommon for library patrons to access these shared cataloging databases because users who were permitted to search the databases had to learn somewhat arcane search commands and interpret MARC record displays. In recent years, both networks have developed front-end software for searching these complex databases (as well as many other databases they have produced or licensed). OCLC has its major database available as *WorldCat* under the FirstSearch service, and RLIN provides its key source through both the Eureka service and the Zephyr Z39.50 method. Both are well-conceived and successful products, but libraries with limited budgets are unlikely to need both. Selectors who are choosing one or the other may find OCLC's database a better choice if they are also conducting most of their interlibrary loan traffic on the OCLC Interlibrary Loan subsystem.

In past years, it was also common for reference selectors to purchase book catalogs for other major research collections, such as the New York Public Library, or for a specialized library with a unique focus, such as the University of Texas Benson Latin American Collection. The latter sort of work can be useful in large libraries as a selection tool for bibliographers and a convenient printed method of seeing one year's cataloged titles in a certain subject area. However, these same bibliographic records are usually available online. For instance, the *Bibliographic Guide to Latin American Studies* currently is compiled from the OCLC records created by the Benson Collection's staff plus online records added by the Library of Congress. Virtually every entry in this bibliography should be searchable in the OCLC system, and the records can be searched in more ways online. Most libraries with access to the online bibliographic networks probably have little need for currently produced library catalogs of this sort.

A question frequently posed to librarians (usually by nonlibrarians) is why a library should subscribe to and search these bibliographic networks for a fee, when a large number of library catalogs are available for free searching through the Internet. This argument makes sense in some particular cases. For example, users who want to see which local library holds a certain book and who are likely to travel to that library to read or borrow it can be better served by searching that one library's online catalog and verifying that the book is not checked out (something the bibliographic utilities cannot do). However, the process of sequentially searching dozens of library catalogs, many with different search software, is a much less efficient use of users' time than is one search in a large common database. Frequently, users will have no idea of which library catalogs might be best for a search, so poor choices are possible. This uncertainty might cause average patrons to pick some of the biggest libraries, leading to the situation in which many people decide to search Harvard's or New York Public Library's catalogs. This puts an extra burden on the carrying capacity of the remote libraries' Internet connections. Thus, for most situations, using the large shared network's common database is more efficient in time and more comprehensive. Modern libraries would be hard pressed to find a reason to avoid offering their users access to OCLC or RLIN.[9]

Subject bibliographies make up the third major category of bibliographies found in reference collections. These are usually monographs that cover some major portion of the publications written about a particular topic. Most cover at least books and periodical articles written about the subject; some include or specialize in covering other media. Reference collection users find subject bibliographies valuable because the tools have already performed the task that the users themselves frequently need to do—compiling a list of potentially useful items on their subjects. Any good bibliography that covers a topic normally selected by the library is a good candidate for purchase. However, some are more appropriate in reference collections than others.

Selectors should look carefully at the scope of a bibliography being considered for purchase. Although the topic may fit within the type of subjects that are usually selected by the library, the topic needs to be one that is sufficiently popular to be useful in reference. A subject bibliography that will be used infrequently, maybe no more than one time per year, is doing little good in the reference collection. The occasional user would be much better off being able to check the book out of the library, if desired. Also, how thorough is the coverage of the topic? Comprehensive sources are generally to be preferred to those with a limited scope. However, in collections serving beginning users, whether the general public, children, or college students, a list of carefully selected sources, representing the compiler's examples of the most-appropriate titles for beginners, can be more useful and more heavily used than a comprehensive, unselective work. Finally, for either the comprehensive or selective subject bibliography, annotations for each entry make a work superior to one without them. Annotations that describe, and perhaps evaluate, each source provide users with more information to guide them in deciding which sources to locate and read.

Indexes and Abstracts

Indexes provide access to the contents of a variety of multipart publications, including periodical issues, books containing several essays, and anthologies of poems and plays. Usually, the most important of these are the periodical indexes, for they function along with the library's catalog as the predominant tools used to locate materials in the library. Periodical indexes are also the resources in the reference department that have caused the biggest change in how librarians and their patrons go about their work. We have moved from the sight of many users poring over volumes among rows of Wilson indexes, newspaper indexes, and advanced abstracting services to that of users searching indexes in electronic formats, sometimes searched from outside the library itself.

The change to electronic formats for indexes has had many ramifications, not the least being cost. A few electronic products may be cheaper in that form than earlier printed versions, but libraries more often are paying additional fees for the digital data, especially if the data are networked and available to more than one user simultaneously. These electronic products are consequently taking up a larger proportion of the reference budget than the printed indexes did. As important as the increased cost is to libraries, the popularity of the electronic indexes is perhaps even more eventful. Many users, especially students who have grown up with the electronic format, are so enamored of using a computer to find their information that they refuse to use the remaining printed indexes in collections. They frequently use online indexes that are less appropriate for their subjects than printed sources that exactly match the scope of their queries. Reference selectors can feel pressured to subscribe to additional electronic sources for specific subject areas so that users receive high-quality assistance.

Furthermore, selectors have many options for providing the indexes to their users. Electronic indexes may be purchased for stand-alone CD-ROM workstations, added to CD-ROM servers for networking, loaded from magnetic tapes onto the library's online catalog system, or accessed remotely through a network or the Internet on a consortium's server or that of a database vendor or producer. The pros and cons of these various formats for different types of reference sources are discussed in the next chapter and compared with traditional printed sources. In some cases, printed indexes may continue to make sense to purchase. When usage for that subject index is not extremely high but subject coverage is still needed for the reference collection, then a good printed index may be the best purchase.

Other than the earlier enumerated criteria for reference sources, such as authority and currency, what characteristics should be evaluated when considering a periodical index? First, the quality and thoroughness of indexing is important. Some publishers have developed a reputation for excellence in choosing appropriate and consistent subject headings as well as in fully covering indexed periodicals. Other publishers are considered by many to be more slipshod, inconsistently following a thesaurus for subject and name headings and not indexing every issue from cover to cover. Second, the selector should consider the match of the index's periodical coverage with what is appropriate for that library. Libraries other than large academic and public libraries may prefer to choose indexes that cover little more than the titles found in the local collection, encouraging maximum use of those periodicals. Other libraries may intentionally want to cover as much of the information universe as possible, perhaps strongly encouraging interlibrary loan for titles not found locally. They are not concerned about an index's match with the local subscriptions. Third, selectors should consider the presence of abstracts. Users have become more accustomed to finding summaries or even the full text of articles and are less satisfied with mere citations. Abstracts provide the user with a way to further assess the value of articles and, in some cases, provide all the information the user actually needs. Abstracts thus serve to save the time of the reader. They may also prevent the staff from spending time unnecessarily processing interlibrary loan requests for items that turn out to be irrelevant to the user's interests.

Handbooks

The handbook is a reference source that is difficult to define exactly. It is usually written on a fairly specific subject area and attempts to provide a basic outline of knowledge for that topic. A handbook in many ways falls between a subject encyclopedia and a textbook. The text is often divided into chapters rather than alphabetical entries. The aim of most handbooks is to provide information at the point of need; that is, they are thought of more as ready-reference sources rather than sources to be read through in a linear fashion. Many handbooks are published in the engineering and scientific areas, and they often serve as desk references for professionals.

Due to their ready-reference nature, handbooks are obvious candidates for a reference collection. Selectors should watch out, however, for those that begin more closely to resemble monographs or textbooks. Those with lengthy chapters and minimal indexing may be rather inefficient reference tools and perhaps are better located in the circulating collection. The narrow focus of many handbooks could also make them unlikely to receive frequent use, so attention to the frequency of reference questions in that subfield should be considered before acquisition. Selectors should note that the word "handbook" is frequently used by publishers in the titles or subtitles of their works, and many of these have marginal value for reference work.[10]

Statistical Sources

In most libraries, statistical questions are exceedingly common. Many librarians would probably agree that a reference collection cannot have too many statistical sources, assuming they are all of good quality. Obviously, accurate and authoritative sources are essential for reference. As previously discussed, library users may accord reference sources additional authority over items found elsewhere in the collection, so it is important to keep questionable or out-of-date statistical materials out of the reference collection.

Because librarians receive so many statistical questions, secondary finding tools that help locate the best statistical compendia for different subjects are quite valuable. Broad secondary sources such as *Statistics Sources* and focused ones like Daniells' *Business Information Sources* can be lifesavers for staff who are asked to find answers for less common queries. A wide variety of these secondary sources exist and, like good subject bibliographies, are excellent for making the search for statistics more efficient.

Another means to efficient gathering of statistics comes from works that compile several years of statistics. For instance, users frequently want to trace figures such as the Consumer Price Index, the population of U.S. cities, and the Dow Jones Industrial Average over many years. It is possible to do so from the annual or more frequent publications to which libraries usually subscribe, such as the *Statistical*

Abstract of the United States. Some of these titles also give some range of historical statistics. However, librarians and users alike are well-served by compendia of statistics covering many years, which cut down the amount of time required to gather the numbers. Although there may be some duplication of information with the frequently published sources, these historical volumes are well worth their expense.

Electronic sources of statistics may also provide increased efficiency of searching. Many business and economics statistics are available from commercial producers, and considerable amounts of data may be gathered from the Web pages of U.S. government agencies. One possible advantage to selecting electronic over printed statistical sources is that some computer-based products will allow users to manipulate the data within the program or to download the data in a format that can be manipulated at the users' discretion. Many programs and Web sites, for example, permit the downloading of data in a format that can be directly inserted into spreadsheet software. Users are able to perform various statistical calculations with these data on their own computers.

Almanacs

Almanacs are small tools that contain a wealth of information, often covering statistics, biographical sketches, noteworthy annual events, sports results, basic data on countries and cities, and much more. Although much of this information can be found in other reference sources, the best examples—*The World Almanac* and the *Information Please Almanac*—cover so much information clearly and inexpensively that they are essential ready reference tools. A number of more focused almanacs are also published and worthy of consideration, if they match the library's collection guidelines: regional titles, such as *The Texas Almanac,* and subject-oriented almanacs, such as *The Nutrition Almanac.* The standard criteria for evaluation apply to any of these titles. In addition, older editions of the major almanacs can provide useful historical information, and much like encyclopedia yearbooks, they offer users an encapsulated, contemporary view of one year's events.

Geographical Sources

The basic reference sources that provide geographical information are atlases, maps, gazetteers, and travel guidebooks. Atlases may be world, regional, subject-based, or historical. They have in common the use of maps to display information about geographic areas. World atlases are the most frequently used of these titles in most libraries, and several high-quality titles are available. Selectors do well in purchasing a variety of these atlases, if possible, because the titles differ in how much information they include and in how they present their data on the page. One title will frame a particular country or region differently from another, and users quite often want to find a particular view of an area of interest (frequently for photocopying purposes). Unfortunately, large world atlases sometimes treat a country or region at a scale that requires the user to look on several pages to see all of that country or region.

Selectors should look for atlases that present their information clearly and legibly. The more comprehensive world atlases may include tens of thousands of place names on their maps; some titles do a much better job of placing all of this text on the maps. Also important is the ease of using the atlas. Some sources provide a logical flow from one page's maps to the next, so the user can easily browse a region for the desired map. Others, however, make browsing difficult and require the user to consult an index or table of contents for the preferred chart.

An atlas's lack of detail is not necessarily a mark against it. As with all reference sources, the intended audience for the tools should drive the decisions on what to purchase. A good number of world atlases provide much simpler maps than the large sources like the *Times Atlas of the World*, which is probably the most comprehensive one-volume world atlas. These simpler atlases may be superior to the *Times Atlas* for younger students in most situations and may occasionally be preferred by adult users who need basic map information. Simpler atlases may have less clutter and show more land area on each map, making orientation and location of major features easier. Again, large collections would do well to include a variety of world atlases, including the comprehensive and the basic titles. Software versions of atlases are another option, but most of those published to date have done a poorer job of geographic visualization than the print sources, providing fewer details and less resolution. CD-ROM or online atlases can usually be manipulated to show and print a user-defined area, which is one of their best features.

Most atlases published today will include a number of thematic maps and often a fair amount of text. Although individuals who own atlases may read these texts, library users appear to do it rarely, making this feature irrelevant. The thematic maps are another issue, however. Atlases that include supplemental maps portraying topology, climate, demographics, land use, and so on are quite helpful and desirable.

Subject or thematic atlases have been produced in considerable numbers in recent years. The best of these sources provide maps depicting historical and cultural developments in a certain region as well as supplemental text and illustrations. Historical atlases are especially useful for students, as these tools graphically depict major changes in borders, migration routes, exploration, results of wars, and other events covered in history classes. Some of the thematic atlases currently published are much less useful, as they consist mostly of photographs and simplistic text. They tend to perform better as coffee table books than atlases. However, a few of the better thematic atlases do provide exceptionally good illustrations of their topics and somewhat more useful accompanying text, and selectors may consider these to be highly illustrated subject encyclopedias.

Maps are, of course, as much a potentially fine source for geographic information as are bound atlases. Individual maps for small areas, such as cities and counties, will often contain much more detail than can be shown in an atlas. Some maps are also updated on a regular basis and are more current than atlases. Oversized atlases can require some planning for shelving, since they often will not fit on regular-sized shelves, but these issues are manageable. Maps present many other problems because of their physical qualities. Folded sheet maps do not easily stay in place on shelves, though labeled file boxes will help. Flat sheet maps require special (and expensive) map cabinets and are more difficult to retrieve and keep in order. Yet the information that only these maps can provide is very useful to most reference collections, and at least some attempt should be made to acquire the most relevant titles. In particular, local maps and city maps for major destinations can easily be acquired and stored in file boxes or filing cabinets.

Gazetteers are geographical dictionaries. They provide a brief description of a geographic site's location and sometimes include additional useful information, such as the origin of its name, pronunciation, population, and former or later names for the same place. Although large libraries will want to acquire many of these, including titles that cover various regions of the world, small libraries may opt instead for a few basic titles that cover major names but are less comprehensive. Selectors should also look for comprehensive sources about their local regions, as many reference questions seek information on regional or state locations. Historical societies often produce geographical sources with this sort of information. Selectors may also consider some or all of the volumes being produced in *The National Gazetteer of the United States of America,* a relatively inexpensive but thorough publication of the United States Geological Survey. Note that most U.S. geographic names can be searched freely at the Geographic Names Information System Internet site sponsored by the U.S. Geological Survey at http://mapping.usgs.gov/www/gnis/gnisform.html.

Travel guides, if purchased at all, are not housed in the reference collection in many libraries, perhaps because users who are taking trips would prefer to check out these books. Yet travel guides can provide a great deal of useful information for the reference collection. Most of them function as very compact directories (for transportation, accommodations, and attractions), encyclopedias (brief histories and place descriptions), and atlases (local maps). When purchasing for the reference collection, selectors should choose from those that appear to have the greatest amount of substantial data about the regions.

Directories

A variety of directories are necessary for those users seeking names, addresses, phone numbers, and electronic mail addresses. Major types needed in most reference collections include directories of city telephone numbers, companies, associations, and schools. Because these sources are used for contacting and locating people or organizations, accuracy and currency are paramount. Most directories are published annually or less frequently, so users are never quite sure that an address or phone number is current. Some duplication of sources in each category may help because they are often published at different times of the year. Selectors should periodically review the sources they have placed under subscription and gather feedback from the reference staff on how accurate and current the sources appear to be. Some directories tend to be less reliable because of their sources; for example, the *National Faculty Directory* compiles much of its data from textbook publishers' mailing lists, and it has not been uncommon to find an address for a person that reflects a university position two or three jobs back. On the other hand, there are no other comprehensive directories for this information, so a selector must weigh the presence of much good data with the existence of some incorrect data. The reference selector should pay attention to the methods and frequency of data gathering used by any directory, especially an expensive one.

Directories represent one area of reference books where print sources are rapidly becoming a second choice to electronic sources. A considerable number of products have become available in the last few years in different electronic formats: CD-ROM directories, such as the *Encyclopedia of Associations* and *American Business Disc,* and specialized business subscriptions with up-to-date contact information plus statistics, such as *Hoover's Online* and Moody's *Company Data Direct.* Even more useful for the average user is the directory information that is available for free over the Internet. Several companies provide address and phone directory information for people throughout the United States via their Web sites, although there is again some question about the accuracy of the data. An increasing number of companies, schools, and other organizations are creating Web sites that give contact information, location, mission statements, and so on. Although there occasionally is a site that does little to update its information, this ability to visit the home page actually maintained by the entity being sought is proving to be an extremely powerful and accurate way for users and librarians to track down directory-type information.

Biographical Sources

Biographical sources are designed to identify people and describe their contributions. Even the most basic biographical source will provide for each entry some personal history, birth and death dates (if applicable), profession, and that person's claim to fame. These sources are especially popular in school and public libraries, where children frequently work on biographical assignments, but they are also well-used in most academic libraries. Biographical dictionaries are usually described according to whether they cover people no longer living ("retrospective" sources) or living ("current" sources), their geographical area of coverage, and possibly their thematic approach (such as biographies of scientists or women). Naturally, there is some overlap among these sources, which is desirable for comparative purposes.

Generally speaking, selectors should attempt to supplement major international and national biographical dictionaries with regional and topical sources that match the interests of their primary users.

Due to the large number of biographical dictionaries, a market in secondary sources has arisen. These tools indicate in which other sources a user can find a particular person profiled. One of the most comprehensive publications, *Biography and Genealogy Master Index,* provides citations to entries in approximately 700 different biographical dictionaries. Although expensive, this title is a major time-saving device in libraries that carry a wide range of biographical titles and want to avoid searching a large number of them. The selection of titles this work indexes can be worthwhile to check against a library's holdings if the library wants to increase the collection's biographical coverage.

H. W. Wilson's *Biography Index* takes a different approach to the large amount of biographical information by offering citations to biographical articles in periodicals, books, and book chapters. The usefulness of this index points out one feature that is very important in biographical reference sources: bibliographic pointers to other information. Many of these tools have brief entries, and users who want more information should be directed to some other sources. Publications such as *Current Biography* and *Contemporary Authors,* which cite other relevant articles on the biographee, are to be preferred over those without such a feature.

Reference selectors should be aware that the popularity of biographical sources with the general public has encouraged the creation of quite a number of rather shoddy reference books in this area. In particular, vanity publications on biography appear regularly, and reference librarians occasionally get on the mailing lists of their authors. Care should be taken in evaluating sources that are produced by unknown publishers or by those known to be second-rate.

Methods of Evaluation

To apply all the criteria and suggestions presented thus far, reference collection selectors must have a way to see and use the prospective sources or to find critical information about the sources. That is, selectors need some information on which to base their decisions.

Personal Examination

Of course, the preferred method for any selector is to be able to inspect the source personally before making a decision to purchase. This is quite easy if the library has an approval plan in place with a vendor. Approval plans send items to libraries based on profiles the libraries establish. Profiles commonly provide for certain subjects at certain audience levels to be sent to the libraries, and they can usually be set up to include or exclude particular publishers. Books arriving on approval offer selectors the best chance to evaluate them according to the reference criteria. Facts can be spot-checked against other authoritative sources, binding quality can be assessed, and clarity of design can be tested.

Some libraries do not have formal approval plans for reference purchases. However, some reference publishers will be glad to send an approval copy of a source at the direct request of a librarian. This is especially true for the "big ticket" items, where selectors are wary of making a mistake and need convincing that the purchase is appropriate. University presses, especially those frequently participating in vendors' approval plans, are less likely to do direct approvals. The disadvantage of asking publishers for individual items on approval, of course, is that the streamlined process of the standard approval plan for receiving and returning books is not in place, so there is some extra effort and cost involved in returning items that are not selected.

Publishers and vendors of online products are willing to allow potential buyers to try out their wares, probably because they are often more expensive than many print items. Most major database vendors will send libraries trial versions of CD-ROM indexes—sometimes these are merely subsets of the main database, but often they will be full versions that must be returned within a short time if not purchased. Likewise, almost all major online vendors have some procedure for trial use of their products. Of course, a great advantage of this method for libraries is that staff can observe their actual user populations using the trial products and giving feedback on the databases' appropriateness and ease of use.

For titles in which obtaining an approval copy or online access is not feasible, the motivated selector has other methods for personally viewing the items. Other libraries in the immediate area can be checked for copies, or any library may be asked to send a volume through interlibrary loan. (However, most libraries will not lend a title that is shelved in their reference collections unless special arrangements are made.) Finally, the local bookstore is often a useful place for personally reviewing recent reference books. Bookstores may not carry some of the most expensive or academically sophisticated reference titles, but a fair number of reference-format titles are in most good-sized bookstores. These stores may be particularly useful for looking at the more popular titles, such as travel books, quotation dictionaries, college guides, and dictionaries.

When all of these methods fail, publishers on occasion will be able to provide physical examination copies of excerpts from their works. Subject encyclopedia publishers have frequently distributed copies of selected articles from new titles, often including a list of every article commissioned for the set. While this does not allow the selector to consider the consistency of the source's efforts and of such features as indexing, a selection at least gives some idea of the depth of coverage, the typical reading level, and the existence of bibliographies.

Some publishers still send sales representatives on calls to libraries, and frequently they can be asked to bring examination copies of special works under consideration for purchase. The usefulness of these visits is variable, depending on the knowledge of the sales staff. Knowledgeable representatives will frankly tell selectors if a particular encyclopedia is written at an inappropriate level for their libraries, if it is a derivative work from earlier publications, and so on. Unfortunately, the presence of these helpful salespeople appears to be declining as publishing houses are purchased and consolidated with larger media and entertainment corporations, which appear to favor general salespeople over those knowledgeable about the book business. Novice selectors will quickly learn which representatives are worth setting time aside to see and which will provide virtually nothing that cannot be read in a brief brochure. At a minimum, however, the selectors can always press the representatives to bring along copies of works they would like to review.

Publishers' Information

Advertising in the rest of society may on occasion be perceived negatively, but librarians are often thankful that reference publishers focus much attention on getting out information about their publications.

Brochures about new titles from large and small companies are prevalent, and these can serve several purposes: alerting selectors to soon-to-be-published titles; giving information such as scope, audience, illustrations, authorship credentials, and ordering instructions; sometimes displaying excerpts that give some sense of format and clarity of presentation; and blurbs taken from review sources. (These are unfailingly positive, of course, but they serve to highlight features of which the publisher is proud, and they can point one toward the original review.)

Publishers' catalogs are another traditional way of locating and finding some information about prospective purchases. Just like the brochures, these vary considerably; some are slickly produced and give extensive descriptions of many sources, while others are more matter-of-fact lists of titles with a bit of description. For many of the largest publishers, their catalogs may only give extensive information about new titles, as their backlists may be too large to allow for much detail on older items. *Publishers' Trade List Annual* formerly served as a useful collection of catalogs, but it has gradually become less important as fewer publishers are included. Today the trend is for publishers to include their catalogs on their Web sites, which does not provide a single collection for reference selectors but does offer the search capabilities and recency of information that online sources can provide.

Reviews

Selectors must often seek out the advice of experts or others who are more familiar with the sources under consideration. Published reviews of reference sources are the most common method to supplement or substitute for any first-hand information. Reference sources from most of the large publishers and many of the small publishers routinely receive reviews in library and book industry serials as well as in some scholarly journals and occasional monographic reviewing publications. Reference books and electronic products are occasionally reviewed in the popular media, such as newspapers and computer magazines, but this is usually for high profile titles only.

However, reviews are not always dependable for indicating whether any problems exist with a reference source. Several writers have looked carefully at the reviews that appear in professional library journals, and their conclusions have pointed out the overwhelmingly positive nature of most reviews. Too little criticism and careful evaluation accompany the descriptions in many reviews, and a significant percentage of reviews fail to make a recommendation for purchase. Additionally, Sweetland in particular found that there was a low level of agreement among different reviews of the same source.[11] Yet there is useful information to be found in reviews, details that may not be apparent from the titles of works or from publishers' sales literature. The best reviews will offer some comparison of a new title with other titles in the field so that selectors can determine whether the new title might add anything to their collections. Even if the review gives only descriptive information and a generally positive review, readers can sometimes perceive the lack of enthusiasm for a work that has nothing wrong with it but that adds little to the literature. Just as with letters of reference for job seekers, a prospect can be damned with faint praise as easily as with negative comments.

Major Review Sources

Mainstays of selection assistance for reference collections are guides to reference sources, which provide annotated lists of major reference tools in all subjects. These guides are supplemented by reviews in library serials that evaluate sources published more recently. The following sections describe these types of review sources and identify the most valuable titles.

Guides to Reference Sources

Reference sources guides provide checklists of potentially valuable tools in various disciplines. Although these guides are not the most current sources for information, they are extremely useful for determining what significant reference tools have been previously published. The best guides also compare the types of information that a user can expect to find in one source versus another. Selectors who need to evaluate the quality of their reference collections and look for gaps in acquisitions will find guides essential. These guides also serve the equally important task of suggesting sources for reference staff to use when answering unfamiliar questions, serving as a supplement to their library catalogs.

The guides listed here are among the most useful of many similar titles. Several other monographic guides to reference sources, including ones appropriate for small libraries and for children's collections, are described in this book's bibliography. Additionally, there are many guides to the literature of different fields, some broad and some narrow, that include reference books among their listings. Selectors can find the titles of literature guides listed throughout the *Guide to Reference Books*.

Balay, Robert, ed. *Guide to Reference Books*. 11th ed. Chicago: American Library Association, 1996.

> This title has been a mainstay of reference lists since its first edition nearly a century ago. The most recent edition covers more than 15,000 titles in all major subject areas. Subject experts in the different disciplines contributed entries and annotations for those sources thought to be the best available reference tools. The focus is directed at sources most useful to research libraries in North America, so many titles would be too scholarly for small libraries. Yet selectors at less research-oriented institutions will be able to choose relevant titles from among the large number of suggestions presented in this volume.
>
> The depth and breadth of sources covered in just this one (rather large) volume makes it an essential acquisition for most libraries. The shortcomings of the *Guide* are few, but selectors should note that the work is dated almost immediately upon publication (the 1996 volume has a 1994 cutoff date for new titles) and that a number of the titles are out of print. Thus it does not take the place of other reviewing media for current titles; it instead provides the background of the best earlier published works. (An annual update of sorts is published in *College & Research Libraries*.) As such, it gives selectors a tool with which to check the quality of earlier collection development for reference. Librarians frequently refer to the *Guide* when they need suggestions on what source might fill a recently noticed gap in the collection.

Lang, Jovian P., ed. *Reference Sources for Small and Medium-Sized Libraries*. 5th ed. Compiled by an ad hoc Subcommittee of the Reference Sources Committee of the Reference and Adult Services Division, American Library Association. Chicago: The Association, 1992.

Recognizing that its larger guide was too comprehensive for the majority of libraries in the United States, the American Library Association created a guide aimed at small and medium-sized libraries. The most recent edition covers about 2,000 titles that serve a wide audience of library users. A particular emphasis in the last edition was to identify works that serve children's reference needs. As useful as this volume is, selectors again need to note the problem with recency. The cutoff for titles in this edition was 1990, so current selection work will certainly need to rely on more than this volume. Selectors should check for a newer edition of this work. The same ALA committee publishes a list of "outstanding reference sources" directed at smaller libraries in each May's issue of *American Libraries.*

Walford's Guide to Reference Material. 7th ed. London: Library Association, 1996– . Vol. 1: *Science & Technology;* vol. 2: *Social & Historical Sciences, Philosophy & Religion;* vol. 3: *Generalia, Language & Literature, the Arts.*

Walford's is the British counterpart to Balay's *Guide to Reference Books.* Formerly edited by A. J. Walford, each of its three volumes now has a different editor. *Walford's* similarly provides lists with annotations of the most useful reference works in all major subject disciplines. This title admits to its British slant, yet there is excellent international coverage and considerable overlap with the titles in Balay. Recent volumes cover more titles than Balay, and the editors have done a fine job of including works right up to the publication date of the guide. *Walford's* publishes a new edition of one volume each year, so a totally new version is available about every three to four years. Thus its cycle of revision is faster than Balay's *Guide.* Large libraries may find that both Balay and *Walford's* are fine guides that will be useful for reference selection and service. Small libraries will find them both more comprehensive in many areas than needed, although there have been "concise" versions of *Walford's* published in the past.[12] On the other hand, those libraries with very strong collections in certain areas may find that these two large guides have not covered some of the narrower-focused sources they might need.

Major Serial Reviewing Sources

In spite of their usefulness, the guides mentioned in the previous section all suffer from a lack of currency; the newest titles being published are not included. Selectors therefore turn to the serially produced review literature for evaluations of newly published materials. The following titles are among the most useful for reference selectors in all types of libraries.

American Reference Books Annual (ARBA). Englewood, Colo.: Libraries Unlimited, 1970– .

ARBA is unique in its attempt to review virtually every reference book published in the United States and Canada during a particular year. Annual volumes have recently included 1,500 to 2,000 reviews of materials published during the previous year (with a few titles for the year before that, if they were published late enough to miss that year's cutoff). Since its beginning in 1970, nearly 50,000 titles have been evaluated. Reviewers include 300 or so contributors who have been selected by the *ARBA* editorial staff; most are librarians or library school faculty. Reviews are generally consistent in length—about 250 words—and usually evaluative as well as descriptive. Rather than making explicit recommendations for purchase, the reviewers indicate the suitability of particular titles for different audiences. Since *ARBA* attempts to cover every new North American reference book, inclusion does not signify any approval of a title, unlike the guides listed in the previous section. Reviewers are encouraged to document the failings of titles, if appropriate, as well as their good points.

A valuable feature in *ARBA* is its listing of citations for reviews that appeared in professional library journals. For each title reviewed, there are usually at least a couple of citations to other reviews in publications such as *Booklist* and *RUSQ*. These citations are added by the editors of *ARBA*, not selected by the reviewers themselves. Of course, the annual publication schedule means that selectors will have already ordered or received on approval many of the reviewed titles before the annual reviews are available.

The editors of *ARBA* have produced various subsets of their review database for special audiences. One annual publication is *Recommended Reference Books for Small and Medium-Sized*

Libraries and Media Centers, which selects about one-third of the titles from the larger volume that are most suitable for nonresearch libraries. Small libraries may find this title works well as a substitute for the comprehensive volume, for both its reduced scope and price. There have also been compilations of the "best" reference works for various time periods, the *ARBA Guide to Subject Encyclopedias and Dictionaries,* and some other spinoffs. Most of these are especially useful when a library does not subscribe to *ARBA* itself or is willing to accept some duplication to have more subject-specific volumes, as might be pursued when branch libraries with a subject focus want to have these reviews at hand.

Booklist: Including Reference Books Bulletin. Chicago: American Library Association, 1905– . Annual cumulations of the reference reviews are available; most recently, *Reference Books Bulletin, 1996–1997: A Compilation of Evaluations September 1996 through August 1997.* Chicago: Booklist, 1998.

Reference Books Bulletin (RBB) is a special insert in this periodical, containing reviews of approximately 500 reference titles per year. The focus is on current sources of general interest applicable to many types of libraries. Because *Booklist* concentrates more on titles for public libraries and media centers, many academic librarians unfortunately ignore *Reference Books Bulletin.* Although it does not cover esoteric titles, reviews in this publication are among the very best in library literature: descriptive, evaluative, and often comparative. Reviews are written by editorial board members or guest reviewers (whose reviews are reviewed by the board members); they are not signed. Most issues include a feature topic, in which more extensive comparative reviews are included. *RBB*'s periodic evaluation of general encyclopedias is detailed, critical, and quite explicit in its recommendations. (However, it should be pointed out that *Booklist* and *RBB* share the policy of printing reviews of only materials that are recommended for purchase; thus no recommendations for avoiding purchase are included.) A fair amount of attention in *RBB* is devoted to electronic resources. A new column, "Reference on the Web," covers Internet resources, and occasionally an article revisits previously reviewed databases for a second look.

Choice: Current Reviews for Academic Libraries. Middletown, Conn.: Association of College and Research Libraries, 1964– .

Choice is perhaps the major review journal for academic libraries. The several thousand titles it reviews each year are often considered prospective core works for undergraduate libraries. Each monthly issue contains a section on reference sources, usually about 70 titles or so per issue. The critiques are written by academic experts, including college and university teachers as well as librarians. Reviews are not typically lengthy, but they are strong in evaluative content. Virtually all reviews end with a recommendation of the audiences for whom the titles are most appropriate. Also helpful is the advertising in *Choice;* because of its prominent position for academic library selection, publishers aiming new reference titles at this market place a good number of descriptive ads in its pages.

Library Journal. New York: Cahners/R. R. Bowker, 1876– .

LJ has a substantial review section, of which less than a dozen in any one issue are reference books. The reviews cover titles that appeal more to a public library audience than to academic library users, though many of the reference titles are scholarly. Publication of the reviews is quite current with the availability of the sources. The reviews are quite short compared with the other major review journals (about 100 to 150 words each), and there is usually limited critical information. Description is good, however, and those sources deemed especially noteworthy are highlighted.

Two separate review columns treat electronic sources. "CD-ROM Review" covers a handful of products each issue, many of them reference titles. Reviews for the discs are a bit longer and more evaluative than those elsewhere in *LJ* for books. "Web-Watch" is written by different people each time and seems to appear about every other issue. Covering one general subject area per article, the column has recently handled religion and writers' sites. It normally reviews two or so Web sites in some detail, giving readers the "bottom line" on a recommendation, and then briefly describes about another dozen related sites.

LJ also publishes special issues related to reference sources. Each April the editors release a list of the best reference titles for the year, similar to the one published yearly in *American Libraries,* which provides a second chance for selectors to check a list of core titles. In November, this journal devotes an issue to reference publishing, including several articles on the topic and a listing of several hundred recent reference titles (which are provided with an index). Although no reviews are included, the extensive list of new titles is valuable.

Reference & User Services Quarterly. Chicago: American Library Association, 1997– . (Formerly *RQ,* 1960–1997.)

RUSQ is the newly adopted name of the principal reference services journal of the Reference and User Services Association (RUSA) of ALA. Each issue reviews half a dozen databases and about 25 new print titles. There is also a "second look" section that reviews a few new editions of major reference works. Reviews in *RUSQ,* though not as long as those in *Reference Books Bulletin,* are substantial and well-done; reviewers, who seem to be mostly academic librarians, write evaluative entries that usually include comparisons with other competing works. The only drawback to this journal's reviews is their limited number. As a quarterly journal, it will publish only 100 to 150 reviews during the course of a year, a rather small selection compared with the nearly 2,000 in *ARBA.*

Rettig, James. *Rettig on Reference.* Detroit: Gale Research, October 1997– . Available online at http://www.gale.com/gale/rettig/rettig.html (for reviews 1995–1997, see http://www.hwwilson.com/retintro.html).

James Rettig's name is nearly synonymous with reference book reviewing. He has published a very large number of reviews in print publications for nearly 20 years as well as written several thoughtful articles about the process of reviewing. His Web-based review site, originally sponsored by H. W. Wilson but recently moved to a Gale Research Web page, continues to provide useful guidance to selectors. Each month Rettig reviews close to two dozen reference sources, including CD-ROM and Web-based tools. Reviews are well-written—the author obviously enjoys having a little fun with the language—comparative, and evaluative. Obvious concern is shown that electronic sources are critically evaluated as thoroughly as print, and thus some of the more poorly executed CDs and Web pages receive unequivocally negative reviews. The Gale Web site incorporates an online index allowing retrieval of archived reviews by various fields, including subject, publisher, author, and others.

Other Serial Reviewing Sources

Several other serials provide occasional reviews of reference sources. However, the following serials cover only a small number of reference titles or are aimed at a selective readership.

Against the Grain: Linking Publishers, Vendors, and Librarians. Citadel Station, Charleston, S.C.: Katina Stauch, 1988– .

Stauch has produced an unusual, quirky, but refreshing periodical dealing with librarian/publisher topics. Although columns frequently appear and disappear, "From the Reference Desk" has recently been giving brief, evaluative reviews of about 13 to 15 titles per issue, often on a related theme or type of tool (for example, monographic bibliographies). Reviews tend to be mostly positive with limited criticism. Any particular issue may also include informative articles on any aspect of reference publishing and how libraries are coping with publishing changes in the electronic world. It is hoped that the editors will continue to occasionally produce a "Reference Publishing Issue" like the one published in the September 1997 issue.

American Libraries. Chicago: American Library Association, 1907– .

AL does not include reviews in each issue, but it does publish the "Outstanding Reference Books" for each year (as chosen by the Reference Sources Committee of the Reference and User Services Association of ALA) in its annual May issue. The selected titles are oriented toward the small and medium-sized library and typically include mostly encyclopedias and dictionaries. The selectors look especially for sources that fill an unoccupied niche in the reference literature.

The Audiovisual Librarian: Multimedia Information. London: Audiovisual Group of the Library Association, 1973– .

The review section of this journal includes reviews of reference titles with audiovisual subjects as well as CD-ROM titles in various subjects. Reviews, written by teachers and librarians, are several paragraphs in length, usually somewhat informal, and yet critical. Negative recommendations were quite obvious in several recent issues.

Behavioral & Social Sciences Librarian. New York: Haworth, 1979– .

Although there are occasional lengthy reviews of Internet sources and some monographs, the reference usefulness of this title is in its bibliographic essays on social science topics, such as "A Survey of Notable Recent Reference Books in Psychology" in a 1996 issue.

The Book Report: The Journal for Junior and Senior High School Librarians. Worthington, Ohio: Linworth, 1982– .

Among the many reviews in each issue, a number of reference titles (print and CD-ROM) are included both in their own category and sprinkled throughout the subject categories. Reviews of about 200 to 300 words are written by school media specialists. Useful description is followed up with a designation of "recommended," "highly recommended," or "optional purchase." The evaluations also indicate the most appropriate grade levels for the works being reviewed.

Collection Building. Hackensack, N.J.: MCB University Press, 1978– .

"Reference Reviews" in each issue reviews 8 to 12 current titles. The reviews are quite lengthy, sometimes up to 1,000 words, but their quality varies a great deal. Only a few recent reviews appeared to be very critical; several were especially superficial.

Computers in Libraries: Including Internet Librarian and CD-ROM Librarian. Medford, N.J.: Information Today, 1981– .

Other than interesting news, the most valuable feature in this title is the column, "Online Treasures," which frequently gives good reviews of Internet resources. Other articles may sometimes review recent developments in online or CD-ROM reference products.

Database. Wilton, Conn.: Online, 1978– .

This journal provides long, detailed, and useful review articles of a few online or Web titles in each issue. Additionally, there is a "Picks and Pans" column with briefer but evaluative information on databases and Walt Crawford's "CD-ROM Corner," which includes excellent, carefully considered reviews of recent discs (some of them reference titles). This is one of the best titles for electronic resources reviews.

Emergency Librarian: The Magazine for School Library Professionals. Seattle: Rockland, 1973– .

A short "Internet Resources" column gives informal comments on and pointers to interesting Internet tools for students, and a software column also provides short, almost always positive reviews of some electronic reference titles. The short book review section will occasionally review a reference book.

Journal of Youth Services in Libraries. Chicago: American Library Association, 1942– .

Each issue's book reviews section contains at least a few reference sources. Professionally written reviews of about 250 words each are written by children's librarians and some academic faculty.

Library Software Review. Thousand Oaks, Calif.: Sage, 1982– .

In addition to short reviews, this title regularly includes in-depth analysis of major software products that are used for reference; for example, a recent issue included a 14-page review of the ProQuest Direct database interface, incorporating several images of screen displays.

Online. Wilton, Conn.: Online, Inc., 1977– .

Formerly a source for information on the traditional online database vendors, *Online* has more recently focused on the Internet. Some reviews of Web sites are included along with occasional book reviews and a large number of explanatory articles on Web technology.

Public Library Quarterly. New York: Haworth, 1979– .

A number of brief reviews suitable for public library collections are found in the regular columns "For Your Reference Collection?" and "Software Reviews."

Reference Reviews Europe Online. Fiesole, Italy: Casalini Libri, 1994– . Available at http://www.rre.casalini.com/RREO.htm (13 Apr. 1998). Also available in print as *Reference Reviews Europe Annual.* Fiesole, Italy: Casalini Libri, 1996– .

This service began as a free English-language summary of the reviews appearing in the German review source, *Informationsmittel für Bibliotheken.* North American librarians write abstracts of 200 to more than 500 reference source reviews each year. The abstracts are short, but they provide description and a summary of each source's strengths and weaknesses. The titles reviewed in the German *IFB* are European in origin, mostly German, and are oriented toward academic audiences. For those who prefer a more permanent record of the review abstracts, the publisher has begun printing an inexpensive version on paper. The online version allows searching by keyword or by the year of the review. Although this review source has somewhat specialized readers in mind, the mere presence of a free Web site that has spawned a printed publication is quite interesting in itself.

RSR: Reference Services Review. Ann Arbor, Mich.: Pierian, 1973– .

RSR does not provide book reviews; instead, many of its articles are bibliographic essays that cover the reference sources for a particular (and usually, focused) subject. Articles increasingly have begun to have a much stronger interest in Internet sites that serve as reference tools.

The School Librarian. London: School Library Association, 1969– .

Emphasizing British publications, *The School Librarian* provides a few critical reviews of reference books and an occasional CD-ROM product among the much larger selection of children's books.

School Library Journal: The Magazine of Children's, Young Adult & School Librarians. New York: R. R. Bowker, 1961– .

SLJ is one of the main library periodicals for librarians serving youth, standing as a counterpart to *Library Journal.* Each issue reviews a large number of books, though only several are reference titles. Reviews, like those in *LJ*, are mostly descriptive and fairly short, but the perspective of children's librarians as reviewers makes these especially useful. Regular features cover CD-ROM titles and Web sites, and an annual article features the best children's reference books of the year.

Science Books and Films. Washington, D.C.: American Association for the Advancement of Science, 1965– .

Oriented toward general adult to children's materials, this journal has well-written reviews on science sources in various media. Reference books are not reviewed in a separate category, except for some general encyclopedias, so selectors must skim the issues for reference works. Each reviewed title is evaluated for its appropriate audience and given a rating that highlights especially good titles.

VOYA: Voice of Youth Advocates. Metuchen, New Jersey: Scarecrow, 1978– .

Each issue reviews titles appropriate for young adults, including a few reference titles in print and CD-ROM (about a dozen total). Signed reviews are about 200 words long, descriptive, and mostly positive. The CD reviews are somewhat longer and contain a summary of strengths and weaknesses for each title.

Notes

1. See, for example, William A. Katz, *Introduction to Reference Work,* 7th ed., vol. 1, *Basic Information Sources* (New York: McGraw-Hill, 1997); Richard E. Bopp and Linda C. Smith, *Reference and Information Services: An Introduction,* 2d ed. (Englewood, Colo.: Libraries Unlimited, 1995), pp. 293–300.

2. Norman Stevens, "Evaluating Reference Books in Theory and Practice," in *The Publishing and Review of Reference Sources,* ed. Bill Katz and Robin Kinder (New York: Haworth, 1987), pp. 9–19; also published as *The Reference Librarian,* no. 15 (1986): 9–19.

3. Jovian Lang, "Evaluation of Reference Sources Published or to Be Published," in *The Publishing and Review of Reference Sources,*

pp. 55–64; David Isaacson, "Literary Style in Reference Books," *RQ* 28 (summer 1989): 485–95.

4. See, for example, Bopp and Smith, *Reference and Information Services;* Katz, *Introduction to Reference Work;* Frances Neel Cheney and Wiley J. Williams, *Fundamental Reference Sources*, 2d ed. (Chicago: American Library Association, 1980).

5. See Kenneth F. Kister, *Kister's Best Encyclopedias: A Comparative Guide to General and Specialized Encyclopedias*, 2d ed. (Phoenix: Oryx, 1994), pp. 23–50, for a detailed examination; and Reference Books Bulletin Editorial Board, American Library Association, *Purchasing an Encyclopedia: 12 Points to Consider,* 5th ed. (Chicago: Booklist Publication, 1996), for a brief but excellent overview of printed and electronic options.

6. The suggestion has often been made that the electronic version of an encyclopedia provides a better index to the printed set than was available in print, thus permitting users to find information in the printed set more easily.

7. Kister, *Kister's Best Encyclopedias.*

8. See "Library of Congress Announces *National Union Catalog* Changes," *Library of Congress Information Bulletin* 49 (18 June 1990): 227.

9. Walt Crawford and Michael Gorman, *Future Libraries: Dreams, Madness, and Reality* (Chicago: American Library Association, 1995), pp. 166–7.

10. For example, in the Trinity University Library collection in early 1998, more than 7,000 titles in this medium-sized collection had "handbook" in their titles, but only about 1,700 had been selected for the reference collection. However, the 1,700 were out of a total reference collection of perhaps 12,000 titles, showing the common use of the word among reference publishers.

11. James H. Sweetland, "Reference Book Reviewing Tools: How Well Do They Do Their Job?" in *Publishing and Review of Reference Sources,* pp. 65–74, also published as *The Reference Librarian,* no. 15 (1986): 65–74; James Rettig, "Reference Book Reviewing Media: A Critical Analysis," *Library Science Annual* 2 (1986): 13–29.

12. *Walford's Concise Guide to Reference Material,* 2d. ed. (London: Library Association, 1992).

ᎶᏬ 5 ᏕᎶ

Selection of
Electronic Resources

Electronic resources have occupied the center of reference selectors'
attention for the past several years. The number of CD-ROM products
is in the tens of thousands; large databases can be loaded onto local
servers, the local online catalog, or accessed via Internet connections
to the servers of consortia, information producers, or database vendors. The Internet itself has grown dramatically as a way of dissemi-
nating and retrieving free and fee-based data. Selectors have a bewil-
dering array of possibilities for selecting and accessing electronic
reference sources.

Unique Selection Issues

In spite of these developments, the basic core of evaluative criteria
used to choose among these sources and methods is still mostly similar to that for print sources. Questions about a source's scope, comprehensiveness, audience, and so on still apply to the information, regardless of its means of delivery. Yet there are new wrinkles in these

choices, for there are indeed some differences between electronic and print sources that create additional layers of decisions.

Product Differences

The most obvious difference between electronic and print sources is that electronic products are accessed through a computer workstation; a different medium interposes itself between the user and the information. Print sources have a medium as well, but we take for granted the ability of most users in a library to handle the technology of the book. (Of course, there are groups of people who find this technology problematic: those with disabilities may find small print or moving a large, heavy index volume from the shelf quite difficult; functionally illiterate people find any sort of text-based technology of limited use to them. Libraries can and do find ways to accommodate these patrons.) Reviews of print publications do, in fact, make reference to poorly implemented aspects of the medium when they criticize the layout of the text, the arrangement of the sections, and the durability of the paper and binding. However, the issues of medium are more challenging with electronic sources because there is less standardization with these products and people have had less time to adjust to the technology. The reference selector cannot look at just the content of an electronic product; consideration of the interface between user and program, the type of platform required to access the source, and the additional costs of this electronic access are all factors that must be evaluated.

A second important difference between electronic and print reference sources is the nature of the library's ownership of them. Virtually all print sources acquired by a library are owned by that library in perpetuity (or as long as the paper lasts). Occasionally print reference tools must be leased and returned to the publisher, but these are few in number. However, the opposite is true of electronic reference sources. Most electronic indexes, full-text databases, and online encyclopedias are leased products. Libraries license the information for the period of time that they pay for the subscriptions. When subscriptions lapse, many of the electronic sources' publishers give no further access to these products. Therefore, libraries are paying for access rather than ownership of the information in the products. This has created problems with how to pay for the products (should funds come out of the materials budget for something not owned tangibly?), not to mention the serious concerns with how information will be archived if no library is allowed to own the data. A related issue is the maintenance of backfiles even when libraries continue their subscriptions. Some database producers have created electronic indexes that access a rolling number of years of data. Libraries may have the current five years on a CD-ROM, but when next year's update arrives, the most recent year bumps the oldest year off the disc. Such problems must be carefully considered before selectors subscribe to electronic products and before they cancel any print versions of the same products.

Cost Differences

The conventional wisdom was that electronic products could be much cheaper than print versions, since the expenses of paper, printing, binding, and shipping would be replaced by more-economical digital distribution—a CD-ROM is much cheaper to duplicate than a thirty-volume paper set of encyclopedias, for instance. However, publishers have not typically followed the conventional wisdom. They have claimed that the basic editorial process makes up the majority of a product's cost, so electronic distribution makes for little savings. Publishers have also tried to price new products to recoup the expense of designing the software that accompanies the sources. The reality has been no significant savings for most electronic products over their print counterparts and, in fact, higher prices for many of them. When libraries network a product or offer multiple simultaneous online sessions, the cost for this electronic product can greatly exceed the fees paid for the print version.

Pricing for electronic sources is unstable at the current time. Publishers and vendors have still not quite figured out how to price their products to offset any potential cancellations of print versions. Worries over diminishing returns from print products or connect-time based database services, such as DIALOG, have led to pricing that many librarians consider exorbitant. Pricing can change rapidly in this world as publishers look at what others are charging and set their prices accordingly. Many pricing options are often available, and these go far beyond the options that ever arose with print subscriptions. Some electronic reference products are priced according to the number of full-time-equivalent (FTE) students or other users an institution has, some are based on the acquisitions budget of the library, some on the number of simultaneous users that will be permitted to access the products, others on whether the product is used on a stand-alone workstation, mounted on a single-building library network, or networked among multiple buildings. Potential cost savings to publishers and vendors from decreasing the number of individual library accounts they must manage has led lately to major price breaks for consortium purchases, so that libraries attempting to find the lowest cost for many electronic products will find them through joint purchases with other institutions.

Selector Differences

Electronic reference sources, by nature of their new technologies, require additional areas of expertise by the librarians who evaluate and select them. The subject bibliographer for history may be able to critically evaluate the coverage and quality of a multivolume bibliography, for example, but is that same selector comfortable deciding between a stand-alone DOS index and one that runs on a UNIX server and allows TCP/IP connections? Libraries need that sort of expertise, so it must come from these same selectors or from technical experts who may or may not have the required competence to judge the subject matter.[1] Demas and others discussed the institutionalization of electronic collection development at Cornell, asserting that proper training and computer workstations were necessary for bibliographers to achieve competence in this new area.[2] This situation involves a major research library, but the need for staff training to cope with selection issues posed by technology is perhaps even stronger for small libraries. Small libraries often do not have systems librarians or other technical staff to consult on these issues. Managers of these libraries should take every opportunity to upgrade the technological competencies of their staff.

The stakes are high when selecting many electronic products. They may cause substantial change in many areas of library operations: interactions with most patrons in the reference area, the demand on technical staff to troubleshoot hardware and software problems, the rebalancing of the acquisitions budget among various subjects, and so on. Online indexes may provide full-text articles for many citations, causing the library to cope with changes in patron use of periodicals and heavy demands for printing. Because the impact of electronic products potentially affects many library departments, some libraries have instituted review committees composed of members from various departments. Cornell University's Electronic Resources Council "assesses the impact of each selection on library policies and operations before it is selected, and determines if the library is capable of handling the resource."[3] A committee that crosses departmental lines allows for dialogue on the impending changes caused by selecting some products and permits staff to prepare properly for implementation. This avoids staff feeling that they have had sources dumped into their laps with no concern for the impact.

Another option is to divide the responsibilities for selecting electronic sources according to the subject and level of the sources. Johnson proposes allowing individual subject selectors to make purchases in the electronic area, assuming that the products fall specifically within that bibliographer's subject area and the impact on the rest of the library is small. Those products that are of interest to two or more selectors, but are still fairly low-impact, would be chosen jointly by those selectors and the price split between the different subject lines. However, sources that are considered more generally applicable to a wide audience and have a greater impact would be selected by a diverse committee, and the funds would be taken from the top of the materials budget rather than any specific subject lines.[4]

The biggest trend in purchasing electronic sources is the acquisition of them through a consortium. As mentioned, publishers and vendors are frequently willing to give substantial price discounts to groups of libraries. (Part of the reason for this is due to actual cost savings in processing the accounts, but a major motivation is the attempt by publishers to increase their market share in large jumps.) The discounts are appealing to many libraries in this era of tight library budgets. However, sharing subscriptions to online resources requires that the participating libraries agree on the titles to purchase. Collection development staff from the different libraries may be asked to provide input into the selections, but ultimately the decisions on which products to acquire are made among the group of library representatives (frequently directors) from the various libraries. The locus of decision making in these situations is shifted from the local library to the group or consortium, which entails a whole new way of thinking about formerly local reference collections.[5]

Criteria for Selecting Electronic Products

All of the criteria used to evaluate print reference sources are valid points to consider when looking at electronic products. However, due to the nature of the medium and the differences mentioned previously, additional considerations become important when selecting electronic sources. The following major areas for evaluation are addressed in the next sections: contents, interface, output options, hardware, software, costs, and vendor/publisher issues. These issues, taken together, can give the selector a good basis for choosing one electronic product over another or for deciding whether an electronic product meets reference collection needs at least as well as a print source.

The selection checklist provided in figure 2 lists each of these characteristics and provides columns to compare two products. In reality, a number of different versions of the same product may be available from different vendors or in different media (Internet or CD-ROM, for instance). Also, several competing products from different publishers may cover similar subject ground and may need to be compared with each other. How would a selector use this checklist to help make a decision? This can vary according to the interests of the selectors. Many selectors will be comfortable noting comments or figures in the appropriate fields, then looking over the checklist and making a considered judgment from those notes. Other selectors find this too vague and prefer a rating system that uses numeric values. They could give a point value to each of the different criteria, then total up the points assigned to each reviewed product. Naturally, some items on the checklist will be much more important for some libraries than will others, so a weighted set of scores would be more useful than giving one point to each criterion on which one product outranks another. A third wrinkle to this process would be to indicate that certain features are not negotiable, that is, that certain criteria must be met for the product to be considered for purchase.

Contents

The most important consideration for selecting an electronic reference product is its content. Even though an electronic index or encyclopedia has an eye-catching and easy-to-use interface or perhaps comes

Figure 2.   *Selection Checklist for Electronic Resources*

	Product 1	**Product 2**
Contents		
Scope	_____	_____
Comprehensiveness	_____	_____
Currency/update frequency	_____	_____
Full-text options	_____	_____
Years of coverage	_____	_____
Archiving/backfiles	_____	_____
Quality of indexing	_____	_____
Abstracts	_____	_____
Connect to local holdings	_____	_____
Stability	_____	_____
Ownership	_____	_____
Reviews available	_____	_____
Interface		
Search engine (local or proprietary)	_____	_____
Search modes	_____	_____
Search languages and methods	_____	_____
Search construction assistance	_____	_____
Online help	_____	_____
Documentation	_____	_____
Error handling	_____	_____
Consistency of interface	_____	_____
Overall speed of search	_____	_____
Ease of use	_____	_____
Output Features		
Clear screen displays	_____	_____
User-changeable displays	_____	_____
General printing capabilities	_____	_____
Print marked records only	_____	_____
Downloading options	_____	_____
Document delivery options	_____	_____
Hardware		
Server processor required	_____	_____
Server storage required	_____	_____
Other server requirements	_____	_____
Client workstation processor required	_____	_____
Client workstation peripherals required	_____	_____

continued

Figure 2. *Selection Checklist for Electronic Resources (cont.)*

	Product 1	Product 2
Hardware (cont.)		
Communication access method	_____	_____
Communication access reliability	_____	_____
Software		
Server software platform(s)	_____	_____
Client software platform(s)	_____	_____
Networkable	_____	_____
Maximum number of simultaneous users	_____	_____
Z39.50 support	_____	_____
Required downtime to upgrade data	_____	_____
Ease of installation	_____	_____
Well-behaved software	_____	_____
Other software required	_____	_____
User authentication provided	_____	_____
Costs		
First year product price, desired configuration	_____	_____
Ongoing product price, desired configuration	_____	_____
Server	_____	_____
Workstations	_____	_____
Network hardware and software	_____	_____
Printing	_____	_____
Other hardware	_____	_____
Other software	_____	_____
Programmer staff	_____	_____
Staff maintenance time	_____	_____
Hardware/software maintenance	_____	_____
Equipment replacement	_____	_____
Savings if print version canceled	_____	_____
Vendor/Publisher Issues		
Vendor financial stability	_____	_____
Technical support	_____	_____
Data collection for use analysis provided	_____	_____
Perceived ease of working with vendor	_____	_____

with a low price tag, content that is insufficient or inappropriate for the library's users should caution selectors against choosing that resource.

SCOPE

What subject does the resource cover, and how well does it meet its stated areas of coverage? While most print sources will describe their scope in the front of the volume, this information is often more difficult to find during an online or CD-ROM search session. Users should be able to gauge what the source covers from the source itself, without relying on external documentation. Additionally, selectors should note whether the electronic version of a print source contains everything that was in the print version. As described earlier, some electronic encyclopedias have been slow to include most of the illustrations that make the print sets so valuable.

COMPREHENSIVENESS

How much of the information within the previously mentioned scope is actually covered in the source? Some online indexes, for example, provide cover-to-cover indexing for every periodical that they index. However, others are more selective, leaving out smaller or news-type articles, obituaries, letters to the editor, and so on. When comparing two indexes that cover approximately the same subject area, it can be useful to run identical searches in each product and see whether they retrieve all of the same articles from the same periodicals.

CURRENCY AND UPDATE FREQUENCY

How up-to-date is the most recent material in the product, and how often is new information added to the database? Users typically think of electronic sources as more current than print versions or CD-ROMs, but this is not always true. Online products, residing on remote servers, may generally be updated more frequently than CD-ROM subscriptions, but the speed with which the remote products are actually updated can vary considerably. Similar indexes, for example, will often show several weeks difference in the inclusion of certain titles into their databases.

FULL-TEXT OPTIONS

If full-text information is retrievable from the product, in what forms is it available and how complete is the coverage? Full-text delivery of

articles tied into online indexes is one of the big trends in current online reference sources. However, some vendors provide just ASCII
text, some provide ASCII text with separate graphics, and others provide some articles as scanned page images. There are trade-offs
among costs, speed of retrieval, and ease of use with these different
formats. Selectors should judge which formats are most useful to
their users relative to the costs of the products. Also important to consider is how well the vendor documents citations and the exact pagi-
nation of the article, which can make it much easier for patrons to cite
the articles.

YEARS OF COVERAGE

If the product is one that is regularly updated, how far back does the
electronic source go? Many online indexes cover only the most recent
years, not going back to the coverage that a print version may have had.
This may be a minor concern with science and technology products,
but the usefulness of information more than ten years old can be considerable for the humanities. Likewise, statistical information for earlier years is quite valuable.

ARCHIVING AND BACKFILES

Related to the years of coverage, what happens to the older data in the
database as new data are added? Some electronic subscriptions are for
"rolling years" coverage; a library subscribes to the current five years,
for example, and when year six is added, year one rolls off the disc.
Does the product provide any means for archiving its older information? Current subscriptions to vendors through the Internet assume
that the vendor or database producer will maintain the backfiles. Is the
library permitted to make any sort of archival backup of the information in case something happens to the currently provided information?
Some products provide only a current version, for example, *Britannica
Online*. With this encyclopedia, the library is always subscribing to the
current articles in the database (plus some retrospective coverage in
the yearbooks). When an article in *Britannica Online* is changed, access to the previous version of that article is gone.

QUALITY OF INDEXING

How well does the database producer index its information? Certain
publishers have a reputation for consistently high-quality indexing,

whereas other products reveal frequent errors. Testing of the product should include a wide range of searches that look at the accuracy of data entry and the application of subject headings.

ABSTRACTS

Does the product provide summaries of its records? Library users are much better served by periodical indexes that provide abstracts. Not only do they give users more information about the content of sources than citations can, but in an electronic product, the abstracts provide additional keywords for searchers.

CONNECT TO LOCAL HOLDINGS

Does the database provide a feature in which users can easily check the local library's catalog to see if an indexed article or book is held in the library? This can be done by several methods—more easily if the database is loaded on the local integrated library system, but also possible through other methods. Some database systems allow a library to download its journal holdings into a file and allow the database software to try matches against it; in other cases, library staff can manually enter titles and call numbers for local titles into a special file. In any case, the feature can be a great timesaver for patrons.

STABILITY

How consistently does the electronic product cover the same subjects and titles? For bibliographic products, some publishers (such as H. W. Wilson) have kept an extremely stable list of indexed titles over the years, while others (especially those attempting to supply full-text sources) have had substantial changes in coverage on a frequent basis. Since indexes are often chosen based on how well they cover a library's subscriptions, frequent changes in an index may be problematic.

OWNERSHIP

Does the library own the data once purchased, or is this only a lease? Archiving of the purchased information is more dependable if a library can maintain the data for which it has previously paid, even if the subscription is terminated in the future. If the annual fee covers access only, selectors must carefully consider what they will do if circumstances cause the cancellation of a subscription. For instance, if a print title was canceled for an electronic version but the electronic version becomes too expensive and is canceled, the library will have nothing to show for those years after the print title was stopped.

REVIEWS AVAILABLE

Are any published reviews about the product available? If so, where? If the product has not been reviewed, are any other librarians willing to supply feedback about their experiences with the product? Internet Listservs and newsgroups can be a good way to gather impressions on products, though it may be hard to judge the rigor of others' evaluations.

Interface

The availability of a reference source in digital form is supposed to make that product more versatile and useful than a print version of the same title. However, abundant examples exist of products that are poorly designed and difficult to use. Beyond looking at the general design of a product, selectors must evaluate a variety of features related to the interface between the electronic data and its users.

SEARCH ENGINE

What type of searching software is used to drive the reference product? Some products can be made available through the library's online catalog, permitting users to stay with an interface that they presumably know well. Other search software has been used extensively in libraries for a variety of products and has been found acceptable by most users. Selectors should consider the advantages of supplying their users with one interface for multiple products, thus requiring fewer software interfaces for them to learn. New acquisitions that use a unique interface and that are not well designed can cause problems for users and create headaches for support staff.

SEARCH MODES

Does the electronic source permit different levels of use for novices and experts? All software should be designed to enable a novice user to use the product with minimal instruction. Yet very simplistic, menu-driven systems can become tedious for experienced researchers. An easy method for the expert user to perform simple searches quickly or to create sophisticated searches is preferred, especially if the reference source is one expected to receive a great deal of repeated use by the same people.

SEARCH LANGUAGES AND METHODS

What methods are offered for constructing searches more complicated than a single word or phrase? Librarians are familiar with Boolean search operators and like to see these present, though there is some doubt about how much any operator other than "and" is chosen by most users. Truncation should normally be an option as well. However, newer developments in search methods have tried to go beyond Boolean searching. There is a growing popularity of relevancy ranking, in which results are ranked according to how many search terms are found and where the terms are located in each matching record or document. Many Web search engines use relevancy rather than Boolean as a default search method, and Internet-savvy users are expecting this in other products they search. Another option is natural language searching, in which the software parses a normal-language question or statement and constructs a search based on internal algorithms.

SEARCH CONSTRUCTION ASSISTANCE

Does the interface provide a structured method for creating a search statement for the user, or is the user left with just a command line for input? Database vendors are now experimenting with options such as workforms with labeled fields into which a user can place search words or software "buttons" that initiate an interview, asking patrons for information and then completing a sophisticated search for them. This assumes that many users do not wish to read accompanying help screens or documentation.

ONLINE HELP

In spite of the knowledge that online help is not frequently used, does the product supply information within the program that permits the interested user to learn more details of using that system? Especially valuable is contextual help, in which a user is given suggestions for what to do based on the exact place that person has reached in the search session. That is, if a search has been completed and the user wants to display the results, a help command at this point should list the options for displaying records or performing a new search. General help menus that have no contextual relationship to the current user activity are a poor substitute for contextual help. Selectors who see little use of online help in their libraries should keep in mind that remote users, or "independent" users as Kluegel calls them, must rely mainly on the product itself for guidance rather than relying on reference librarians or printed documentation, and they will value online help much more than in-library users.[6]

DOCUMENTATION

Does the electronic product also come with clearly written instructions on how to use the software? Some documentation is abysmal, giving only the barest gleanings of how to use basic features and providing no substantial help on advanced functions. Besides in-depth guides to the product, shorter brochures or "cheat sheets" of basic commands can be useful for librarians to copy and disseminate to classes or to immediate users in the reference department. The instructions for installing the software should be distributed separately from those for using the product because many libraries may prefer users to remain ignorant of how to uninstall the software or override printing restrictions.

ERROR HANDLING

Does the software provide useful descriptions of user errors, enabling the user to modify the action properly? Those who have been around these products for a number of years remember all too well error messages such as, "Fatal Error 359." Well-written software of the present generation will tell the user what operation could not be completed and what the user may wish to do at this point, all in nontechnical language. Also, errors should be trapped sufficiently well by the software that users are not dumped out of the program when they choose an incorrect operation.[7]

CONSISTENCY OF INTERFACE

Do the screens flow logically from one to the next, and do users find the same types of features on each screen? The software will be much simpler to use if users can find the commands and features they need, and a consistent use of layout, menus, and display can significantly aid this.

SPEED OF SEARCHES

Are searches completed and results displayed in a reasonable amount of time? With CD-ROM databases on local hardware, it is easy to test a product and judge its speed relative to a certain type of workstation. This is more difficult with online sources, since the speed is affected by the throughput of the communication line and the load on the remote server. Yet repeated testing of a reference source should enable selectors to judge the acceptability of response time. User frustration can become quite high when response time is inconsistent and slow, so special care needs to be taken to ensure that a product can deliver respectable performance under different loads.

EASE OF USE

When looking at the interface features, as well as subjectively reflecting on the search experience, is the software relatively easy to use? Software that requires frequent instruction by a librarian or the invoking of online help gets in the way of the content, which is, of course, the reason a product is chosen. Much of this judgment will be subjective, and selectors in the same library may prefer one interface over another. However, selectors should be able to reach a reasonable consensus on the best and the worst products.

Output Features

Reference books and serials have traditionally been evaluated for the clarity of information on their pages. However, the quality of their screen displays is only one of the output characteristics that should be reviewed for electronic sources. Users not only read from the screen but also like to print and download information from these titles.

CLEAR SCREEN DISPLAYS

Are the screens highly legible, directing users to the important information? A graphical user interface has the potential to be very clear and attractive, as well as cluttered and confusing.

USER-CHANGEABLE DISPLAYS

Can the user make some changes to suit his or her preferences? For example, indexes should permit various formats of records to be displayed, from brief title listings to citations to full records with abstracts.

Changeable fonts and sizes of typefaces can make the screen easier to read for some patrons, including those with vision difficulties.

GENERAL PRINTING CAPABILITIES

How well-designed are the printing options? Even with more and more information being displayed on video screens, users still want to print out the citations, data, or article text retrieved from the databases. Can the software print selected text from the retrieved results or merely entire records or screens? As with screen displays, users will sometimes want to configure what prints and how it looks on the page, so the ability to change these options suits many users.

PRINT MARKED RECORDS ONLY

Can a user select or tag certain records and then print only those records? Librarians who monitor paper usage and printing costs need to have some methods for eliminating wasteful printing. Software that permits the printing of only selected records can lead to substantial savings for a library over time.

DOWNLOADING OPTIONS

Can users download to either fixed disks on their own machines if they are connected remotely or to diskettes if they are using library workstations? The ability to download can provide users with the opportunity to take the results and manipulate them further on their own workstations, while also saving printing costs. Some software can be configured to prevent downloading to the local hard drive, which libraries find useful for preventing users from inadvertently copying their information to the library PC rather than their own diskettes. Also, can the data be downloaded in formats that match the possible uses of the data? For example, financial statistics from an electronic business source might be usefully entered into a spreadsheet or database program. Can the software download the data in formats other than plain text for importing into those programs?

DOCUMENT DELIVERY OPTIONS

Can the program send results to a user via electronic mail? The ability to do this in OCLC's FirstSearch databases has been a popular feature with users, and just like downloading, it offers libraries another way to discourage excessive printing. Many online databases now offer users the capability of ordering full documents via the online system in those cases where the local library does not own the material or when the remote user does not want to go to the library to retrieve the item. Useful options for this feature include ordering with a personal credit card as well as an option to order from the library's account. In the latter case, some libraries have canceled print subscriptions to journals and offered campus users free ordering of any articles they need that can be found in the online source (for instance, using CARL's UnCover service). Libraries will need procedures to limit this to only preselected user groups, such as faculty.

Hardware

Books and printed serials might be said to have associated hardware costs: Shelves, tables, chairs, and light fixtures, for example, are needed to house and read these materials in the library. However, electronic products need these types of items as well as sophisticated computer hardware for storing the data, if done in-house, and for providing user access to it. These hardware items can make up a substantial portion of the entire cost of offering the products.

SERVER PROCESSOR REQUIRED

If the software is loaded on local hardware, what type and level of computer processor is necessary to run the programs? Currently, much of the development of software for library database applications is going toward either Intel processors running Windows software or these and other processors running UNIX software. Library staff need to determine what level of hardware is necessary to support the expected use of the server and then size the processor(s) and other hardware appropriately.

SERVER STORAGE REQUIRED

What hard disk space, number of CD-ROM drives, and tape drives are necessary to handle the volume of data that will be loaded on the server? In the last few years, hard drive prices have dropped dramatically as drive speed and capacities have leapt ahead. Electronic products that are shipped on CD-ROMs to the library and were formerly mounted in CD drives are more frequently being loaded onto hard drives for faster access. With some large databases like MEDLINE taking up many gigabytes of storage space, appropriately sizing the needed storage space is important.

OTHER SERVER REQUIREMENTS

Are additional hardware items needed to run the intended software, including additional peripherals, controller cards, backup devices, universal power supplies, and so on?

CLIENT WORKSTATION PROCESSOR REQUIRED

What types of workstations in the library and at remote sites will be able to access the database? As microprocessors have increased so quickly in speed and power over the last few years, the new software has been written with the expectation of running on the newer, more powerful processors. Thus many libraries find that they need fairly current, high-powered PCs to run their reference applications successfully. At the same time, a few vendors, such as ABC-Clio, Wilson, and SilverPlatter, have attempted to maintain software that will run on the older, slower equipment that many libraries still possess.

CLIENT WORKSTATION PERIPHERALS REQUIRED

Do users' workstations need to be configured with any additional equipment to operate the software? Stand-alone CD-ROM programs, of course, require a CD-ROM drive connected to the local machine; some software permits updates to the CD database by using a modem to connect to the most recent data available from the publisher. A local area network used for reference resources may require network interface cards in each client workstation.

COMMUNICATION ACCESS METHOD

If the reference source is loaded on a server, what telecommunication method is used to connect to the server? Internet-based databases require some sort of connection to the Internet, either through dedicated Internet lines or dial-up accounts through the local phone system. Larger-scale access to the Internet will involve the purchase of communication cards, routers, and so on.

COMMUNICATION ACCESS RELIABILITY

Can the server be reliably accessed from the users' workstations? Local area networks tend to be fairly reliable if designed properly. Accessing databases at remote sites, especially when using the Internet, is much less dependable. As Internet usage has expanded quickly in recent years, the amount of traffic on telecommunication lines has sky-rocketed, and response time for users has often slowed significantly. Is the access method one that will provide adequate reliability, especially in light of the importance and use level of the product?

Software

Electronic products employ a wide range of software for interacting with users. Features such as compatibility with existing hardware and software, capabilities for networking and remote access, and ease of installing and maintaining the software can make the difference between a product that is accepted easily and one that creates headaches for staff and users alike.

SERVER SOFTWARE PLATFORM(S)

If the electronic database is mounted on local hardware, what type of operating system is required to run the software? Many products in the past have required loading on either a local mainframe computer or a UNIX-based server. Many currently available products will run on Windows NT or NetWare servers, which are more manageable for many libraries. The level of staff computing expertise and the presence of systems people available to the library will help determine what platforms can be supported by the library and, thus, what electronic reference sources can be acquired.

CLIENT SOFTWARE PLATFORM(S)

In past years, much of the development of electronic reference products has been in the Microsoft DOS/Windows area, requiring libraries to purchase PCs that supported this software. Some vendors have provided client software that works with multiple platforms; SilverPlatter, for example, has long provided client software for DOS, Windows, Macintosh, and UNIX workstations. A recent trend has been that of making products available through the Internet, using any one of the popular Web browsers as the client software. Because Web browsers are available for all of the major platforms and are usually free to libraries and individuals, they provide a convenient way around the software platform issue.

NETWORKABLE

Is the product one that can be networked at all? Libraries may not want to spend extra funds to network some products, but in other cases, the anticipated demand makes this feature important.

MAXIMUM NUMBER OF SIMULTANEOUS USERS

If the software is networkable or available online, there is usually not a predetermined hardware/software limit on the number of users that can access the database. Usually, this limit is part of the contractual agreement when the product is acquired. How many users can access a product at the same time based on this contract? An important feature is some method of disconnecting users after a period of inactivity. A search session that has been abandoned but not shut down may prevent another user from using the software for an indefinite amount of time. Many online and locally networked programs have a time-out feature that can be set to end a session when the software senses no activity for a certain length of time, for example, 15 minutes.

Z39.50 SUPPORT

Does the reference product have the ability to be searched by another program using the Z39.50 standards for information retrieval?[8] Although this international standard has not yet been heavily implemented as a standard for searching, more and more reference products and online catalogs are offering this support. A product that supports Z39.50 can use another search engine to search its data by using the remote search engine's interface rather than that of the local product. Users can then search multiple databases with the same interface.

REQUIRED DOWNTIME TO UPGRADE DATA

Does the local system need to be shut down to perform either data or software upgrades? System downtime for upgrades will limit the number of hours that a library's users will be able to search the system. Software that permits routine maintenance to be performed while the server is kept running is preferable to that which requires the server to be shut down.

EASE OF INSTALLATION

How easy is it for staff to install the software and any upgrades? Does the installation process require little staff expertise, or does it involve extensive knowledge? Many libraries without much technical expertise on the staff will have problems with more complex software.

WELL-BEHAVED SOFTWARE

Related to the ease of installation, how well does the product work with other software on the workstations or server? A number of CD-ROM programs in the past have required various configuration changes on individual workstations, such as changing values in the "config.sys" file. Making these types of changes can sometimes result in other software not working properly on that workstation. Well-written programs make no changes to the basic configuration of the computer on which they are installed.

OTHER SOFTWARE REQUIRED

What other software might be required for the product to be used fully? For instance, ProQuest Direct from UMI provides page images for articles, but users must display these files with the Adobe Acrobat software. Certain U.S. government CD-ROM products require the use of database software to produce anything but the simplest data display. Will users have access to the necessary additional software, and will staff be able to instruct patrons in how to use it?

USER AUTHENTICATION PROVIDED

If an online service requires verification that a user is connecting from an authorized account, does it provide a simple way to do this? Many databases currently available via the Internet permit users into the system based on their workstations' IP numbers, which reveal whether the users belong to a subscribing institution. This is a simple solution, though it does not solve the issue of how members of the subscribing institution who are off-site users can access the resources when they use a different Internet service provider. Other products require users to sign in with an ID and password, which can be problematic for libraries with many user groups to manage. Does the software provide some method of scripting password access for workstations within the library?

Costs

The purchase or subscription price for an electronic product is only the beginning of expenses for that title. Just as books take up shelf space and require staff processing, so also do CD-ROM and online resources require disk space and significant staff support. Electronic products also require potentially expensive workstations and networking hardware for them to be used by library patrons.

FIRST YEAR PRICE FOR DESIRED CONFIGURATION

How much will a subscription or purchase of the product cost when simultaneous access for the desired number of users is configured?

ONGOING PRODUCT PRICE FOR DESIRED CONFIGURATION

How much will additional years of this acquisition cost? It is not uncommon for costs to vary between the first and subsequent years, even disregarding normal price increases from providers. Some products will cost more during their first year, due to one-time expenses for backfiles, etc., while others will cost less as their vendors give a discount to encourage new purchases.

SERVER

Will the product require the purchase of a new server or an upgrade to one the library already owns? Server costs include additional disk space that may be required to load another product as well.

WORKSTATIONS

If the current number and type of workstations in the library are not sufficient to run this product, how much will it cost to equip the library properly? This may require purchasing new computers or upgrading those presently owned.

NETWORK HARDWARE AND SOFTWARE

For any but stand-alone installations, libraries may need to install network cards, cabling, and other hardware and software to enable connections to a remote server.

PRINTING

Will the library provide printers with each workstation or some shared printers? Free printing will incur significant annual costs in paper and toner or ink, and charging devices placed on printers to recoup expenses are an expensive initial outlay.

PROGRAMMER STAFF

If the installation of electronic products is sophisticated, involving server setup, systems staff may be needed to install and maintain the equipment and software. Even if this is done with internal systems staff, the time taken to perform these services is still an expense for the institution in terms of time taken away from other potential services.

STAFF MAINTENANCE

What other staff time must be devoted to keeping the system running, upgrading the data, and other maintenance activities? For instance, an inexpensive CD-ROM product at the Trinity University library requires a complete reinstallation of its software each time an updated disc arrives at the library, and on occasion the upgrade has not gone well. The low outlay for the subscription is partially offset by the amount of staff time taken to make the product available to users.

HARDWARE AND SOFTWARE MAINTENANCE

What expenses must the library pay for regular maintenance on its equipment and software? Many institutions place their equipment under maintenance contracts to cover normal breakdowns and repairs. Network servers may also require maintenance fees for the network software. Each additional workstation added to the library will increase the likelihood of repair expenses in any given time period.

EQUIPMENT REPLACEMENT

How long will the current equipment last before it needs to be replaced? Current developments in personal computer hardware make machines obsolete in an increasingly short time. Libraries may want to budget for a three-to-five-year replacement cycle for their workstations, if possible. Of course, many libraries do not have the flexibility to replace machines this often, and some electronic reference products will continue to run on machines older than that. Printers will also tend to wear out in a few years and should be considered consumables, rather than long-term capital acquisitions.

SAVINGS IF PRINT VERSION CANCELED

If the library decides to purchase an electronic product for which a print version has been under subscription, how much can the library save by canceling the print version? The reference selectors may not wish to get rid of the print version, and those reasons may take precedence over cost savings. Some publishers will give a sufficient price discount for subscribing to both versions so that the savings from canceling the print are small. Yet most libraries will experience significant savings by subscribing only to the electronic versions.

Vendor and Publisher Issues

Librarians have frequently chosen book or serial vendors based on the quality of their services. Electronic products require additional levels of support, including technical assistance with installation and maintenance and improvements or corrections to software. Because libraries often invest considerable effort and funds in the provision of these products and the reputation of the library may be affected by their successful implementation, librarians have strong incentives to look carefully at their vendors' financial stability and commitment to service.

VENDOR FINANCIAL STABILITY

Is the vendor in good financial condition and able to fulfill its obligations? Vendors that appear to be doing business effectively are more likely to enhance and upgrade their products, provide appropriate support, and develop additional products. This issue may be a critical one when a library changes its most heavily used reference titles to digital versions. A vendor's poor performance can lead to serious problems with the source's delivery, which can cast a negative light on the libraries subscribing to the product.

TECHNICAL SUPPORT

Does the vendor supply technical support for all hours that the library staff might wish to use it? Is the quality and responsiveness of that support worthwhile? Most libraries will run into occasional unsolvable problems with electronic products. A vendor that supplies limited technical support hours or is unable to answer technical questions in a timely manner can be problematic for a library.

DATA COLLECTION FOR USE ANALYSIS PROVIDED

Does the vendor provide some form of data collection for gathering statistics about the use of the product? Selectors who want to judge the amount and types of use that a source is receiving can benefit from reports that show how many users did how many transactions over a set time. For those libraries that offer substantial resources to remote users, statistics that show how much of the use was outside the library can be helpful. Some online vendors of periodical indexes are able to provide information on the number of retrieved citations (and full-text articles, if available) for every title covered in the database, which can provide useful statistics for bibliographers in various subject areas.

PERCEIVED EASE OF WORKING WITH VENDOR

Does the vendor go out of its way to satisfy its customers and provide an effective product, or does the vendor show little concern once a product has been sold? Reference selectors who have dealt with many vendors and publishers of electronic products develop a sense for the ones that are most likely to ensure satisfied librarians and library users. These vendors are responsive to reports of problems, listen seriously to suggestions for improvements in their products, and are willing to customize aspects of the product or the price if warranted.

Electronic Reference Sources versus Print Sources

What of those situations in which an electronic version of a reference source is available to replace an existing print source in the reference collection? Those of us especially in academic libraries hear a strong preference for electronic products from our students and from at least some of the faculty. Are electronic versions of these tools always to be preferred over their print counterparts? When we look at how these media compare on some of the key criteria for effective reference sources, print sources, in fact, often come out as the better value.

For instance, consider the user's access to the material. The printed volume is limited to just one user at a time, making simultaneous access to the information difficult. Of course, multivolume sets of encyclopedias and indexes can be used by more than one person at a time as long as the demand is not for the same volume. Print sources must also be used physically where that copy is located. Obviously, electronic products that can be networked or made available on the Web can reach many people simultaneously (if their licenses permit it) and remotely, so that users need not be where the data are stored. However, libraries experience times when their online products are not available: servers crash or need maintenance, the Internet is responding sluggishly if at all, or perhaps all library workstations are in use with other products. In these situations, a printed volume can be much more dependable than the electronic versions. For key reference sources like encyclopedias and dictionaries, a library may find it most helpful to its users to keep at least one copy of them in paper format.

Ease of use is another critical factor for which we evaluate reference products. For large data files, such as periodical indexes, an electronic version can be vastly easier to use. The searcher can look through multiple years with a single search statement, matching keywords in different record fields and limiting by language and format, if desired. Other than familiarity, there is little reason to prefer a print index over an electronic one. However, this assumes that the software provided with the electronic version is well-designed and user-friendly. Most of the products that libraries acquire do seem to be at least relatively easy to figure out after a few minutes, but some publishers have developed electronic versions of their products using what must have been a lowest-cost option for search software. This search software is sufficiently difficult that even reference librarians repeatedly refer to instructions or help screens. Users may actually prefer a printed product over these poor implementations.

Additionally, quick searches for a discrete bit of data may sometimes be simpler with a print tool. For example, *Britannica Online* is an excellent online encyclopedia that includes a dictionary as well. For remote users, this offers reference sources right on their desktops. In the library, however, students who want a quick definition or a person's date of birth will more often than not turn to a print copy of a dictionary or encyclopedia rather than launching a Web browser, entering their search words, and waiting for a response. This also appears true for basic directory information sources. Although many libraries subscribe to CD-ROM or online business sources, and excellent Web sources such as Hoover's, Inc., provide some free information, there is no major drop in the number of users who still refer to print copies of the Hoover's handbooks or Standard & Poor's directories. For a quick handle on a company's line of business, address, or major financial statistics, users in the library find that print resources still work well.

What about the ease of reading the material online? Print periodical indexes have never been among the most readable of publications, so indexes that are displayed on the computer screen are not harder to read. In fact, the ability to choose a large font with most electronic indexes makes them somewhat more readable. However, other types of reference materials do not transfer so well to the screen. As Crawford and Gorman note, the resolution of the better computer monitors today does not measure up to the resolution possible on the printed page.[9] Graphical images tend to suffer on the screen as a result. Thus information providers have two main options: make an illustration or map about the size of a typical computer screen and put less information on that graphical image than the print source would have in the same space or create much larger images that require the user to scroll about the image to see it all. The first option has been the path taken by many of the electronic encyclopedias; illustrations—and maps, in particular—tend to be much simpler and less informative than those in the print versions. Those that create the larger-sized images require users to pan about the image, which can make it harder to comprehend what is in the image because the user loses some contextual information when seeing only a portion of the image at one time. Thus some graphically rich reference sources, such as atlases and heavily illustrated encyclopedias, suffer from being put into electronic format.

Electronic reference sources can, of course, include types of content unavailable in print. Animation, multimedia, and hypertext are all intriguing elements that reference sources can put to good use. The ability to see the movement and hear the sounds of an animal, rather than just seeing a static photograph of it, greatly enhances the information that the user receives. Yet some electronic sources have not made extensive use of this technology. The earliest CD-ROM encyclopedias contained only text without graphics. *Britannica Online* has been criticized in past years for its lack of graphics, though it has greatly increased them recently. The first CD-ROM version of the *McGraw-Hill Encyclopedia of Science and Technology,* a profusely illustrated print set, left out more than 75 percent of the illustrations that appeared in the paper version. Selectors should therefore look carefully at the content of digital versions of traditional reference sources and evaluate whether the sources have omitted anything in the move to the computer.

Previously mentioned is the concern about the permanence of information that a library receives in electronic form. Whereas the purchasing library has owned almost all print materials, most electronic sources are leased and must not be used if a subscription lapses. Cancellation of an electronic product usually means that the library loses the entire backfile included with the product. There is also concern among some selectors that even titles that they own may not be permanent, due to the uncertainties of the technologies. CD-ROM technology, for instance, is often considered a temporary technology that will give way to other media in the near future. What will happen when CDs have no longer been manufactured for many years, the library's CD drives no longer work, and those products are not owned in any other format?[10]

Finally, electronic products may be more costly for libraries than their print counterparts. Even when an online or CD-ROM version is cheaper than the print equivalent, the library must factor in the costs of additional workstations, server storage space, printing costs, and other hidden costs. Selectors may often need to choose a print product over an electronic product in the interests of the library's budget.

For at least the near future, then, the real benefits of paper publications over electronic products will mean that reference collections will contain a mix of formats. Decisions will continue to be made based on what serves the library's users best with the most efficient use of funds. Print reference sources are by no means obsolete in the current world. For some applications, paper still outperforms electronic media. In fact, in conversations with publishers at national conventions, most of them believe that they still have a strong market for print resources, and they are continuing to develop new titles at a rate similar to that of the recent past. The number of reference books showing up in comprehensive review sources such as *American Reference Books Annual* has shown no indication of dropping precipitously. If there is a complete shift away from some types of print reference sources in the near future, it will most likely be a cessation of print periodical indexes, which represent one type of tool for which the computer performs much more effectively.

Integrating Electronic Resources into the Reference Collection

If the reference world for the foreseeable future will contain several media types, including print and electronic, it is important to integrate the new technologies with the old. Otherwise users may overemphasize the importance of the flashier electronic resources and diminish the importance of print collections. Integration of electronics and print begins with the collection development policy and procedures of the library, as discussed in chapter 2. Selectors need to consider any new acquisition according to its potential to serve reference functions for the library's users, regardless of its format. Reference librarians should be included in any discussion of adding electronic resources or canceling or weeding print resources, for they are in the best position to realize the impact that such changes will have on patrons. Demas has frequently made use of the term "mainstreaming" to emphasize the importance of not taking the new electronic sources out of context, but instead placing them within normal collection development and management processes—processes that should expand to cover the new format.[11]

The organization of the reference collection has an impact on how successfully electronic products are incorporated into it. This organization has both a physical, tangible element and an intellectual element. The physical location of digital sources in the library has an effect on how patrons will use the materials. It is highly preferable to locate reference workstations in the immediate vicinity of the rest of the reference collection and the reference staff. Doing so provides a link with the traditional reference sources and allows reference staff to help advise users on the best resources for their queries. On the other hand, some libraries have installed banks of workstations in another room or another area of the library. Library users who gravitate toward those remotely placed electronic products will be even less likely to receive suggestions on which resources to use, and they may never make their way to the reference desk area where reference librarians could guide them to appropriate online resources and help them make effective use of the products. For educating users about which sources serve certain purposes best, there is no better method than the mediation of reference staff.

The intellectual challenge to organizing electronic resources into the reference collection includes alerting users to all of the resources that are available, while doing so in a consistently understandable way. Paper volumes are organized logically in a reference collection, and once users learn this system, they will have a sense of where to look for business information or literary criticism sources, for example. However, as Kluegel points out, the mental map that users make of a physical reference collection is no longer available when the user moves into the electronic realm.[12] Almost all reference librarians will recognize the scenario in which a user believes that a certain resource is always located on a certain computer at one location, failing to understand that a networked resource may be available from any of the workstations in the area. Other users fail to note the difference between a library catalog terminal and a CD-ROM workstation. The computer workstation itself does not always carry any obvious identification of what it contains, so users either are baffled by what they might find or create their own mental maps of what they think should be there.

Staff need to offer techniques that help their users create mental maps of the new resources. A simple solution that worked in the past was to label workstations so that users could distinguish PCs or terminals devoted to different resources. In the early years of automation, when catalog terminals replaced card catalogs in the same location and a few CD-ROM workstations could be placed near the print periodical indexes, the connection of the new products to the old was fairly clear. However, given the number of electronic products available in many libraries today that can be accessed from any PC, these labels do not make much sense. Any workstation might be able to connect to the library's catalog, search some networked CD-ROM databases, retrieve a full-text journal article, or search the Internet.

When the options for source selection become plentiful, libraries are frequently using menu systems on their workstations to guide users toward the most helpful choices. Some libraries have incorporated a large number of resources into their online catalogs that give users a central starting place with pointers to various resources, including periodical indexes, online encyclopedias, and Internet links. Perhaps the most common technique now being pursued is the use of Web pages to outline and structure the world of available information for library users. Many libraries are using the Web to describe their collections and services, and the Web pages also contain selected pointers to resources outside the library's collections. Some libraries are using their Web pages as a way to guide and instruct their users through the process of finding information, including both print and electronic resources. For example, Ohio State University Libraries currently have a "Gateway to Information" project that guides users from their topics through a several-step research process, offering examples of reference sources in print and online formats along the way.[13] Attempts such as these put the various formats into context rather than merely listing a mélange of resources under no organizing principle. Users can begin to see how the electronic resources fit in with the rest of the library's reference collection.

An additional concern of reference librarians is the effectiveness with which patrons use these electronic products. No one will argue that library users always made the most effective use of the print reference sources, but there is also the sense that the limited search options that can be performed with a print reference source can be understood fairly well by users. However, the search software available with many electronic products allows much more sophisticated searching compared with that of print sources. How can library staff determine whether the electronic titles they are acquiring are actually being searched well by the users? Some form of follow-up by reference staff seems appropriate to ensure that users are not getting lost or choosing the first and easiest material they can retrieve. There are several options for this follow-up: analyzing transaction logs, if available, or any other statistics provided by the resources; gathering feedback from users, such as testing students on their searching skills; and simply asking questions of users as they search the products.

Integrating the Internet into the Reference Collection

Many new electronic reference tools have been developed and acquired over the past few years, but the developments receiving the most attention are those concerning the Internet and, in particular, the World Wide Web. The amount of information available through the Web has been growing at an amazing rate, and reference librarians and teachers find that many students turn first to the Web for information rather than to traditional library materials. Useful information, provided by governmental and professional associations, commercial firms, and even individuals, is indeed available. However, anecdotal discussions among colleagues indicate that students have a difficult time discerning which material on the Web is valuable and credible and which is unworthy of consideration. In the deluge of hype about the Web, reference librarians are concerned that users will be unable to judge when they might profit from using the Internet and when they would be better off using other reference sources. If the Internet is to be integrated into the reference collection, librarians must find a way to help users find the good information that is out there and put it into the context of what else the library can offer.

There are many commercial attempts to index the Web and provide guidance to users. Familiar Web tools, such as Infoseek and Hot-Bot, provide machine-gathered indexing information about Web sites and allow searchers to use various keyword methods to retrieve links to them. Yahoo and Magellan, as well as some other services, also provide human-generated directories of sites that have been gleaned by their staff. According to Rettig, the result is that most commercial indexing attempts to date have been either undiscriminating in their choices, indexing any Web sites that can be found or else selecting sites because of the way they use the technology rather than because of any useful, authoritative information.[14] At this time, librarians will have to create their own pointers to solid reference sources on the Web if there are to be many useful guides for users.

Demas makes the strong point that one of the most distinguishing characteristics that librarians add to the entire information process is selectivity.[15] That is, as selectors for libraries, librarians choose the most useful materials from among all the items that are available; collection development provides a filtering mechanism. Rather than attempting to catalog the Internet, which is a grand idea but probably an unrealistic one to tackle, librarians should be deciding what is valuable on a title-by-title basis and "acquiring" these Internet sources for their collections. Reference selectors should be frequently searching the Internet for information sources that fit the criteria for electronic reference products, then using appropriate methods to make these sources known to users. Whether the items are added to library Web pages or actually included in the library's online catalog, those high-quality sites of information should be incorporated into the basic tools that libraries provide patrons for finding information.

Is giving up on cataloging the entire Internet a position that will make libraries irrelevant? There are certainly questions today about how relevant libraries will be to the next generation, leading some to call for our full efforts toward managing the Internet's resources. However, it is unlikely that libraries will find the financial resources to take on a project of this size. Perhaps it would be better for commercial entities to take on this indexing of the Web, much like commercial firms now produce indexes for periodical literature.[16] Just as a professional association or a private publisher decides to produce an index of psychological journal articles, a similar organization might produce an exhaustive index of reputable psychology sites on the Web. Of course, the organization would need to hire staff to perform this enterprise, and costs would be passed along to libraries that decided to purchase this indexing. The production of major reference tools to the Internet is probably beyond the scope of most libraries today, given their staffing patterns and tight budgets. The best approach may be to participate by finding and indexing high-quality sites.

Where does the reference librarian and selector enter into this picture? The role of the reference selector will probably in some ways stay similar to what it is now, except that the selector will be attempting to acquire the most appropriate reference tools to the Internet along with other reference sources. Just as selectors choose among various commercial and professional periodical indexes now, they will choose the best Internet reference tools. Some of these will be free sources on the Web, perhaps constructed by an interested scholar or librarian, and others may be commercially produced indexes in print or, more likely, electronic format.

For the integration of the Internet with reference collections today, however, selectors must look at the reference tools that are currently available on and for the Internet. The Internet itself contains a number of reference tools of variable quality:

search engines that, as mentioned, are best for inclusiveness and not selectivity, including sources like AltaVista, HotBot, and Infoseek[17]

search directories that show some attempts at human categorization and selection, such as Yahoo and Magellan[18]

current-awareness sources, which highlight particularly interesting Web sites, such as the University of Wisconsin's *The Scout Report*[19]

"FAQs," or frequently asked questions, that are files that give the basics on a particular subject that is a focus of a Web page, newsgroup, or discussion list[20]

newsgroups and discussion lists that often are monitored by subject experts who respond to requests for information

librarians' lists of the most useful Internet resources found on
their libraries' Web pages

print publications about the Internet, including review columns in
library journals and professional books[21]

Careful selection (and maintenance, of course) of Internet resources, incorporated into the guides and even catalogs that librarians
devise for the use of patrons, will help those users understand what
dependable Internet tools are available for them to use and how
these tools fit into the other research tools that reference collections
offer.

Notes

1. Cheryl LaGuardia and Stella Bentley, "Electronic Databases:
Will Old Collection Development Policies Still Work?" *Online* 16 (July
1992): 62.

2. Samuel Demas, Peter McDonald, and Gregory Lawrence, "The
Internet and Collection Development: Mainstreaming Selection of Internet Resources," *Library Resources & Technical Services* 39 (July 1995):
277.

3. Demas, McDonald, and Lawrence, "The Internet and Collection
Development," p. 278.

4. Peggy Johnson, "A Model for Improving Electronic Resources
Decision-Making," *Against the Grain* 8 (Apr. 1996): 16.

5. Kathleen Kluegel, "Revolutionary Times," *RQ* 35 (summer
1996): 454.

6. Kathleen Kluegel, "The Reference Collection as Kaleidoscope,"
RQ 36 (fall 1996): 9–11.

7. Veronica Harry and Charles Oppenheim, "Evaluations of Electronic Databases, Part I: Criteria for Testing CDROM Products," *Online
& CDROM Review* 17, no. 4 (1993): 218, 222.

8. For some background on Z39.50 protocol, see United States Library of Congress, *Z39.50 Maintenance Agency Home Page* (Washington,
D.C.: Library of Congress), online, available http://lcweb.loc.gov/z3950/
agency/ (28 Apr. 1998).

9. Walt Crawford and Michael Gorman, *Future Libraries: Dreams,
Madness, and Reality* (Chicago: American Library Association, 1995),
pp. 19–21.

10. Chuck Hamaker, "Selecting CD-ROMs for Academic Libraries," *Against the Grain* 7 (Apr. 1995): 23–4.

11. Demas, "The Internet and Collection Development," p. 275–90.

12. Kathleen Kluegel, "Finding Our Way," *RQ* 36 (winter 1996): 169–72.

13. Ohio State University Libraries, *The Gateway to Information* (Columbus, Ohio: Ohio State University Libraries), online, available http://www.lib.ohio-state.edu/gateway/ (2 May 1998).

14. James Rettig, "Beyond 'Cool': Analog Models for Reviewing Digital Resources," *Online* 20 (Sept./Oct. 1996): 56–60.

15. Samuel Demas, summarized in Maggie Bartley, "Report of the ALCTS New England Collection Management and Development Institute, July 27–29, 1995," *Library Acquisitions: Practice & Theory* 20, no. 2 (1996): 173.

16. My first concept of this scenario was based on the comments of a Trinity University colleague, Clare Dunkle.

17. *AltaVista: A Digital Internet Service,* online, available http://www. altavista.digital.com/; *HotBot: the WIRED Search Center,* online, available http://www.hotbot.com; *Infoseek,* online, available http://www.infoseek. com (all 2 May 1998).

18. *Yahoo!,* online, available http://www.yahoo.com; *Magellan Internet Guide,* online, available http://www.mckinley.com/ (2 May 1998).

19. Internet Scout Project, Computer Sciences Department, University of Wisconsin, *The Scout Report* (Madison, Wisc.: University of Wisconsin), online, available http://scout.cs.wisc.edu/scout/report/ (2 May 1998).

20. *Usenet Hypertext FAQ Archive,* online, available http://www. faqs.org/faqs/ (28 Apr. 1998); see also Russ Hersch, *FAQs about FAQs,* 17 Nov. 1997, online, available http://www.faqs.org/faqs/faqs/about-faqs/ (3 May 1998).

21. A new title that I have not yet viewed and that looks very valuable in this context is Shirley Duglin Kennedy, *Best Bet Internet: Reference and Research When You Don't Have Time to Mess Around* (Chicago: American Library Association, 1998).

ᐒ 6 ᐓ

Practical Procedures

Careful selection of reference materials, although crucial, is only the beginning of the reference collection management process. Staff must also choose the most efficient methods of acquiring these titles, including the development of approval plans and standing orders. Collections must then be periodically evaluated to see how well they serve their intended purposes, and those titles that no longer contribute to these purposes should be removed from the reference collection. The practical procedures involved in the acquisition, evaluation, weeding, and maintenance of these resources may be less glamorous than purchasing the materials, but these procedures are essential to creating an effective reference collection.

Acquisition

Selectors for the reference collection decide what to acquire, but other library staff usually are responsible for ordering the sources and seeing that they are processed and cataloged upon receipt. Most libraries have in place typical mechanisms for ordering books and serials, and increasingly they have prepared procedures for acquiring electronic sources. Procedures need not be extensively different for reference sources as contrasted with other purchases.

Books
APPROVAL PLANS

Monographic publications may be ordered individually, title-by-title, but most medium and larger-sized libraries work with approval plans.[1] As mentioned in chapter 4, approval plans with book vendors allow a library to establish a profile for all the subjects for which it wishes to receive books. The approval vendor then regularly ships an assortment of sources to the library; selectors decide which ones to keep, then send the remainder back to the vendor. There are quite a few major vendors for North American publishers; others specialize in books from other countries. Depending on the size of the library's acquisition budget, the library may elect to use many different vendors for different types of materials, greater discounts, or faster delivery.[2]

Approval plans are designed to ensure that libraries receive the majority of relevant publications for which their collection policies call, while permitting staff to review the sources and decide whether to keep them. This is especially valuable when the sources are expensive, as many reference titles are. Approval plans allow more efficient paperwork for receiving, returning, and paying for materials as well as making it easier to stretch the library's spending through the entire budget cycle. Most approval vendors provide a standard discount for items purchased through them, passing along some of the discounts they receive from publishers. Finally, receiving items on approval offers libraries the chance to let selected users give their opinions on purchase. This is common in academic libraries and is usually restricted to faculty. (Of course, letting faculty give their input can sometimes be problematic if they recommend buying books that are outside the normal collection scope. If the approval plan is well-targeted to the library's needs, this problem should occur only infrequently.)

Some thought must be given to how reference materials are arranged for the review of approval books. Arrangements must be made to ensure that the selection of reference titles and the decision to place them in the reference collection are made by those assigned to manage that collection. When sorting titles for review, staff must decide whether approval books that are reference-format titles will be shelved by themselves or with other books on the same subject. If they are arranged by subjects, the selectors with responsibility for reference will need to go through each of the subject areas and choose which titles should go into reference. Another option would be for each subject selector to make his or her purchase decisions on likely titles for reference, then move the items to another shelf for review by the reference selector. Certainly, subject selectors may be given the authority to make these decisions, but as noted in chapter 3, this then removes a large portion of the new titles from the oversight of the reference selectors.

Unfortunately, approval plans cannot be counted on to fill all of a libraries' selection needs because a significant number of titles will not be covered under any approval plan. Occasionally, approval vendors may elect not to handle a particular title. More likely, vendors will not be able to acquire books from certain publishers. Many research centers, government agencies, small presses, and industry self-publishers do not make their titles available through approval vendors.[3] Some of the major reference publishers also refuse to participate with approval vendors, or they may eliminate most or all of the discount that vendors need to make a profit—effectively removing themselves from the approval plan. Other publishers will normally provide materials to vendors, but they may elect to pursue sales of a potential bestseller on their own and avoid the cost of working with the approval vendors for that title.

Approval plans are also offered directly by a few publishers of reference books, who will ship each new title (or in some cases, just new editions of previously chosen titles) to a participating library and allow the titles to be returned for no charge if unwanted. This may be useful for libraries that select a large percentage of those publishers' titles. However, the acquisitions process is usually more efficient when these publishers are consolidated with other publishers in a larger approval program.

STANDING ORDERS

Standing orders are another method of automatically receiving books and serials from publishers. While they are more often discussed in terms of serials, standing orders can be established for the books of certain publishers. Unlike an approval program, this sort of publisher-direct standing order results in nonreturnable items coming into the library. This method can be useful, nonetheless, for less mainstream publishers, such as local chambers of commerce and government agencies, from which the library may want to purchase everything possible.

FIRM ORDERS

A firm order is a direct request to purchase a title; it almost always requires the library to pay for the item when it is received. (Returns are accepted by most publishers or vendors for good cause.) Rather than being able to review the book in hand before making a decision, selectors making firm orders base their decision to purchase on other information. Even in libraries with major approval plans, a significant amount of firm ordering takes place. Libraries can order directly from publishers, or they may order from a vendor or "book jobber" that carries a large selection of titles from many publishers.

Firm ordering reference titles through vendors offers many of the same advantages as the approval plans: consolidation of paperwork for ordering and billing, potential discounts off the list prices, and frequently, faster delivery of the books to the library. The main drawback is the inability to browse the sources in person before selecting them. While most selectors will not worry too much about acquiring an inexpensive source that turns out to be a disappointment, they will have more concerns when the unseen title is several hundred dollars, which is not unusual for many reference titles. As a result, selectors should investigate expensive titles that are not being received via approval as carefully as time permits, looking for reviews and any opinions of librarians who have already purchased the titles.

Sending firm orders directly to publishers is warranted in several situations. Some of the less mainstream publishers will again be sources not covered by the vendors. In some situations, publishers offering prepublication prices at substantial discounts to the list prices will provide a better discount than that offered by the vendors, who may not receive any additional discount from the publishers. This will frequently be true as well for publishers offering sales on their backlist catalog, who are trying to move out older inventory. Although vendors pride themselves on service, there may be the occasional case in which a publisher can supply a copy of a book needed "rush" faster than the library's vendors are able to. Only experience in ordering from a variety of sources will yield such comparative information.

Serials

SUBSCRIPTIONS

Reference serials, including periodical indexes in print or electronic formats, annuals, looseleaf business sources, and so on, are by nature items that come out sequentially and are thus usually ordered by subscription. As with books, serials can be ordered through a vendor or directly from publishers. Using serials vendors is strongly preferred over individually ordering titles through publishers. Vendors not only consolidate subscription orders and bills but they also provide other features that make work simpler for librarians. Serials publishers often run behind on their publication schedules, and vendors will provide claiming of missing issues. Foreign publishers are easily paid through the convenience of a vendor in one's own country, simplifying currency exchange. Price discounts are sometimes available from vendors, though the discounts are not as substantial or common as with books. Major vendors also collect statistics on price increases by their contributing publishers and provide reports of these increases to libraries so they can estimate future budget requirements.

APPROVAL PLANS

Although most periodicals are not covered by approval plans—subscriptions do not provide an item-by-item return option—some annual reference works can be acquired through them. This is especially helpful when a selector does not want to acquire, for example, every issue of a directory that changes only in small percentages in any one year. Some vendors will establish standing orders for titles, in which a notification form is sent whenever the new volume is available. Libraries may then send in the form to receive the volume on approval, or they may decide to wait until another year and merely toss the form away. This standing order on forms arrangement is quite helpful as a reminder to check up on titles not purchased every year.

FIRM ORDERS

Most serials are ordered on subscription, not on a volume-by-volume basis. However, there will be occasions when selectors would like to have a current copy of a serial reference title and they do not wish to initiate a subscription or receive every volume. Most publishers and vendors can provide a single volume for these titles. Libraries can save the recurring cost of a subscription for an item that may need replacement only every two, three, or four years. (Of course, considerations of the information's currency must be addressed in these cases.)

Allocation of Funds

The way in which a library assigns the cost of reference materials to particular budget lines is frequently problematic. This problem once again relates to the issue of whether reference sources are treated by their subjects or their formats; that is, should an item be charged to the reference budget or, say, to the business budget line? Further complications arise when the source is electronic and the library has a separate budget line for electronic reference sources. Should a new business directory on CD-ROM be charged against the business line, the reference line, or the electronics line? In some libraries that are fairly flexible with their budgets, the problem is not a large one. However, many libraries use rigid funding allocations for departmental lines, and in these situations, the application of costs to the proper budget line can be a political problem.

One possible solution is to charge all reference purchases to the subject areas. That is, a book or CD-ROM or online database related to business would be charged to the business line of the library budget. However, some reference titles cover many subject areas; into what subject would a selector place a general encyclopedia or a multidisciplinary online periodical index? For those who wish to continue allocating funds just to subject areas and not by formats, a "general" budget line may cover some of these titles.

Perhaps more useful is providing the selector(s) in charge of the reference collection with a separate budget line for reference materials. Besides allowing a place for more multidisciplinary titles to be charged, creating a reference budget line also permits the reference selector some independence in ordering new materials. A particular title might not be ordered by a subject bibliographer, but the reference selector may determine that it would be used frequently in reference and should therefore be acquired.

Of course, creating a separate budget line for reference can cause other questions to surface. Will all materials of reference format be charged to the reference line, or only those items that are eventually added to the reference collection? That is, if the title is ordered as a reference source but, upon inspection, is thought to work better shelved in the circulating collection, does the reference budget still pay for the source? What happens when a subject selector misses or intentionally passes on acquiring a source that the reference selector wants to add; against which budget line will this title be charged? If the reference budget is not sufficient to pay for every reference title the library acquires, how is the decision made on whether to charge reference or the subject for each title?

Setting up allocations in any one manner will not create perfect solutions for these questions. One way to work through some of the concerns is to establish that the reference line will pay for any general works or works that cannot easily be classified into a single discipline. All other reference titles would be charged to the appropriate subject lines. Multidisciplinary works could have their costs spread among the several subject lines that have some connection to the subjects covered in these reference titles. One further method is to split the cost of especially expensive reference titles, such as major subject encyclopedias, between the applicable subjects and the reference budget line. All three of these methods are workable in some library situations; again, the flexibility of the collection budget and the relative politicization of the budget process will help determine how easily any particular one may suit a given library.

Assigning New Titles to Reference

Reference selectors should help develop a procedure at their libraries to determine how a newly received source in the acquisitions department will be designated as a reference book. Titles ordered against the reference line may usually be assumed to be headed for the reference collection, but a review by the reference selector may determine that the title is more appropriate for the circulating collection. Quite a number of titles that arrive in acquisitions after having been firm ordered by various subject bibliographers turn out to be more reference-like than may have been thought at the time of ordering. Thus there needs to be some method for catching these titles before they all end up in the circulating collection (or before every reference-looking title is sent to reference).

Two simple steps can improve the likelihood of catching these titles. First, ordering procedures can be set up so that selectors who make the firm orders can designate on their orders that particular titles should be considered potential reference books. This will alert acquisitions staff to handle these items differently when they arrive. Second, acquisitions staff should be trained to look for new titles that could be reference sources but that were not specifically ordered as such. Acquisitions staff should take both titles from both these situations and place them in a review area for the reference selectors to evaluate. For example, Trinity University routinely places firm-ordered materials that are potential reference titles on shelves near the approval books. During the same period in which approval books are marked for approval or rejection, bibliographers check these shelves and determine whether any of the sources are suitable for the reference collection. After review by the head of reference, the firm orders are taken down and processed at the same time as the approval shipment.

Of course, the occasional book is missed, and a title suitable for the reference collection is inadvertently placed in the circulating collection. This can be rectified when a staff member or user notes the misassigned location and brings it to the library's attention. Procedures should be put in place to determine how this request for relocation is initiated and who has the responsibility to do so.

Evaluation

Selectors always have the best intentions when adding titles to the reference collection. These new sources are chosen to help users and librarians in solving their reference needs. However, as time goes by, parts of the collection can become dated, other areas may have received less attention but now need more because of changes in user needs, and good potential selections may never have been acquired. Thus, any reference collection must be regularly evaluated to ensure that it is still performing its reference functions successfully. Several evaluation methods, both formal and informal, can be used to ascertain its quality.

Feedback from Reference Users

Since the reference collection exists to serve the needs of individual library users, perhaps the most useful evaluation tool is to obtain users' opinions about the collection. Patrons frequently speak with reference staff about what they have found that works well, what they would like to find but could not locate, and what they found that did not suit their needs. Sometimes it is the savvy library user, perhaps a faculty member at a college or a retired person doing local history research at the local public library, who alerts the staff to the absence of sources for certain subjects. The reference staff should carefully note whether library users are solving their queries with the sources available in the reference collection. If not, staff should record these queries and determine whether the needed sources are indeed absent from the collection or whether that particular user had difficulties locating sources that are present in the collection.

Of course, this form of feedback is anecdotal, not scientific. First-hand descriptions of problems are an excellent way to spot-check certain parts of the collection, but they cannot be generalized to the entire reference collection because users are not reporting on using the entire collection. More scientific methods of assessing user success are possible. Biggs reports on several methods of interviewing and surveying library users to evaluate reference collections. However, in the long run, quite a few problems prevent these techniques from giving a completely accurate picture of collection use and user satisfaction. For instance, Biggs points out that interviewed users often want to appear to be sophisticated patrons, and they may therefore report use of materials that they did not actually use.[4] People surveyed may fail to remember or note all materials they used, and they may not give information that helps assess exactly how valuable certain sources were.

Reference staff are also users of the collection, and their feedback is very useful in evaluating the collection. Every time a librarian attempts to solve a user query provides an opportunity to observe whether the reference collection offers a solution. Over time, staff will usually develop a feeling that certain sources work well for reference service and others rarely seem to be needed. Again, this information is anecdotal and selective, and the apparent lack of usefulness of some sources may reflect the staff members' lack of familiarity with those sources. This first-hand data is perhaps the best indicator of which sources are most useful, and the method is less accurate for determining which sources have little value.

When reference transactions obviously fail or are only partially successful, writing down the problematic query and consulting with other reference staff can be extremely valuable. Later discussion may lead to the conclusion that the reference collection does not own a source that handles the problem, and selectors can attempt to acquire a source or sources that will improve the collection in this area. Another possibility, of course, is that helpful sources do exist in the collection, but that a particular librarian was unfamiliar with or forgot about that source. Thus this sort of record keeping for unsuccessful reference interviews serves to evaluate the sufficiency of the collection and to educate reference staff about items in the collection or about ways to improve their reference interviews.

Note that feedback from library users and staff about the sources that they found helpful tends to give the most information about sources that were used and very little information about sources that were not consulted. Managers of reference collections can learn from this feedback that some sources are valuable and should be kept in the collection, but there is almost no way of knowing whether many, or even most, of the items on the shelf (or available on workstations) are ever used by anyone. Use studies, discussed in a following section, attempt to fill this gap in knowledge.

Comparing the Collection with Lists

Perhaps a more objective method of evaluating a reference collection is to compare what is currently held in that collection with lists of the best reference sources. A number of these lists were mentioned in chapter 4, including publications such as *American Libraries* and *Library Journal,* which routinely list the best reference sources of the year. Organizations such as the Reference and User Services Association (RUSA) of the American Library Association bestow annual awards on reference publishers for distinguished publications, such as the Dartmouth Medal (for outstanding and significant reference works) and the Denali Press Award (for outstanding reference works specifically about ethnic and minority groups in the United States).[5]

Reference guides, also described in chapter 4, can be useful tools for evaluating a collection as well. The large guides, such as *Guide to Reference Books* and *Walford's Guide to Reference Material,* allow selectors to review titles under various subject categories and check their own match with these lists. However, the lists are so large that very few libraries would own most of these titles. Although much of the professional reference literature appears written for research-library audiences, most libraries in the United States are relatively small. Thus a more useful approach might be using the selective guides that are oriented toward medium and smaller-sized libraries, including school media centers. A number of these guides are listed in the annotated bibliography at the end of this book. Also helpful are guides to the literature of a particular discipline, in which an author compiles both reference and other titles that are most useful for studying in that subject area. These guides may go into substantial depth, so selectors will need to choose appropriately to match their collection's level.

Attempts have been made in the past to ascertain the best or key reference sources, those that should be in every collection. Were there a proven list of this sort, evaluation would be much easier to do. In 1991 Hopkins reported on several attempts over the years, some of which included surveys of library school faculty and others that looked at the titles included in major reference textbooks. He concluded that there was a definite lack of consensus for all but a handful of titles, and these few titles hardly constitute even a small reference collection.[6]

Comparing the Collection with Those of Other Libraries

The quality of a publication is not necessarily related to its popularity or amount of sales. Yet there are times when a selection or weeding decision can be influenced heavily by whether a title is in the collections of other libraries. Selectors are aware of a number of libraries with which they compare their own library, a set of peers. Liberal arts college libraries may look at other liberal arts institutions; Association of Research Libraries members will look at other ARL libraries. When it is difficult to decide on purchasing a certain source based on the information that has been retrieved, selectors may check to see if their peer libraries have decided to purchase the title. This can be especially helpful when the source in question comes from an unknown press and no reviews of it are found. Ownership of the title by several reputable libraries may help selectors decide that the source is worth taking a chance on. The lack of a substantial number of titles in one's local library that are found in highly perceived peer libraries may indicate that there has been inattention to some parts of the collection.

How does one get this peer library information? Obviously, checking online catalogs or library holdings on one of the national bibliographic utilities (such as OCLC and RLIN) is quite straightforward. For larger selection projects, libraries can consider purchasing electronic compilations of the holdings of their own library and a number of self-selected comparison libraries, which will permit one library to see how it compares in both the number and identity of titles in various subject areas.[7]

Studies of Use

Getting feedback from librarians and users is helpful, but it is far from scientific due to its subjectivity. Comparisons with published lists of reference sources or with the holdings of other libraries are more objective, but they compare the collection to others that may not have the same types of users with the same needs. Therefore, they should be considered suggestions, not requirements, of titles to own. Managers who have attempted to add more concrete information to the evaluation process have often resorted to use studies of the reference collection.

Use studies attempt to pinpoint which sources are used by a library's clientele and which are not. Quite a number of techniques are described in Biggs's overview of the subject, in addition to the interviewing technique described earlier. Popular ones have included "touch" methods, in which something is added to each book, which is presumably disturbed whenever the book is used; reshelving counts; self-reported use by patrons on questionnaires; unobtrusive observation; and reports from reference librarians about what they use.[8] Biggs points out that each of these comes with its own set of problems, so caution is needed in interpreting the results.

Counting the items that need to be reshelved is one of the most popularly reported methods. The most common techniques involve simple tallies on a sheet when items are reshelved, usually making marks in one of several call number ranges, and "dotting," in which a colored, adhesive dot is affixed to either the spine or the inside cover each time a volume is reshelved. Engeldinger and Sendi both report on use studies in which their staff used the dot method and made evaluations of the reference collection based on the subsequent counting of those dots.[9] Drawbacks to this method, however, include the discipline required to affix the dots consistently to all used materials and the extensive amount of time needed to review and count the dots on the sources.

The rising presence of online circulation systems and bar-coded collections should allow staff to use handheld scanners to collect and count this reshelving information more easily.[10] A two-year study by Welch and others at the University of North Carolina at Charlotte demonstrated this method.[11] In the study virtually all materials reshelved over two years were scanned, and the data were downloaded to spreadsheets that allowed analysis by both individual title and class number. Reference staff then used the data for assistance in a major weeding project as well as an aid for purchasing newer titles in heavily used areas and deciding when some titles could be sent to the bindery with the least likelihood of inconvenience to users. The study's authors felt that the considerable amount of time spent on the data gathering and analysis was justified by the results.

Electronic reference sources offer the possibility of calculating use more easily. Many Internet-accessible tools, such as the OCLC First-Search and the UMI ProQuest databases, can provide subscribing libraries with counts of patron searches and other statistics. Networked electronic indexes on local systems may be set up with software that measures the number of uses, the number of simultaneous users, and so on. Even very basic menu software can permit a reference department to track the number of times a particular CD-ROM product was accessed.

Of course, evaluators must always remember that reshelving counts are never totally accurate because many users will replace volumes themselves and eliminate some counting of uses. A use of an item does not necessarily mean that the use was successful, that the reader found what was sought; a user might go through several different sources before finding the answer, yet all of the sources are statistically viewed the same. A further problem is that users may not choose the best sources for their queries, so a title receiving frequent use may do so only because it is somehow more easily found or remembered by users. The data may suggest that users need information in a particular subject area or in a certain format, but they do not always indicate that the "best" titles, as chosen by experts, were consulted. Biggs sums up this difficulty by pointing out that all of the techniques give some useful information and all have major limitations, causing any careful selector to try a variety of methods to validate one result against those received from other methods.[12] If staffing is insufficient, however, using the direct feedback of users and librarians will often give a good picture of how the reference collection is used. This may be more true in medium and smaller-sized libraries, where the collection is smaller and more easily roamed by staff, than it is in very large research library collections, where users may more easily slip in and out of the area. Feedback must be supplemented with a steady program of weeding out obsolescent resources, however, because the reference staff may not realize when users are attempting to meet their needs through outdated sources.

Weeding

Weeding is sometimes also called deselection, deacquisition, or book retirement. These terms all point to the same concept—the removal from the collection of items not serving the collection's purposes. The term "weeding," however, works well because it includes the connotations of managing an organic, changing subject that must be regularly maintained or else it will suffer from overgrowth and the choking out of useful items. Weeding should not be considered a reversal of the selection process or an admission of having made mistakes. It is instead a normal part of maintaining a vital, functional collection. As the background clutter is decreased, the collection is thereby made easier to search by patrons. Weeding also removes any useless or dangerously misleading materials from the collection, items that look useful by their location in the collection but are in fact outdated, incomplete, or perhaps just quite wrong.

Opposition to Weeding

Although weeding may seem like a reasonable task, many librarians and library users are opposed to any significant levels of weeding. Slote lists several of these reasons in his standard text, *Weeding Library Collections:*

> librarians are afraid of decreasing, or told not to decrease, the volume count of the library for political reasons
> weeding can take considerable staff time and is usually a low priority
> staff cannot agree on the criteria to follow

once in the collection, items acquire almost a "sacred" character
the public, which doesn't understand the reasons for weeding, will
be upset with this perceived squandering of resources[13]

Thus it is incumbent on any reference selector who initiates weeding in a library that has not been doing this regularly to gain the support of library colleagues and management for carrying out the process
appropriately.

What Should Be Weeded?

Simply put, sources should be weeded from the reference collection
when they no longer meet the original criteria for adding them to the
collection. To give selectors the benefit of the doubt, it can be assumed
that all sources currently in a reference collection were originally appropriate selections. What then has changed in the period between the
sources' acquisition and later, when they are candidates for weeding?
The most likely change is due to the age of the material.[14] As a reference source gets older (assuming it is not perpetually updated by a
looseleaf or online service), the information in it is no longer recent.
For some materials, there may be no significant change in the information covered in the sources, so this matters little. However, for most
subjects, new information has been created, new discoveries have
been made, new names are now famous, and so on. Even more important, some of the data in the sources are not only historically dated
or incomplete but may now be incorrect. Thus, as the currency of a
source lessens, its authoritative character also begins to diminish. At
this point, the staff does a disservice to its users by leaving these materials in the reference collection.

Lack of use may also make sources weeding candidates. A source
that may have been heavily used at one time may become relatively
unused later. This may be because the source has been ignored in favor of a newer source that is more popular with users (because it is better, easier to use, or newer-looking), or perhaps because the subject it
covers is no longer as popular with users at that library. Another possibility is that a reference selector misjudged the item's expected use.

Staff who are weeding the reference collection should therefore be
looking for sources that are no longer used much or, by virtue of their
age, have become outdated. Naturally, this process will be easier if it is

performed on a regular basis. Engeldinger points out that "crisis weed-ing" is likely to occur when librarians wait until they have run out of room in a section of the reference collection. At that time, choices are not always made as consistently as they should be, and there may be a tendency to weed from those areas in which the most new titles are be-ing added. Such weeding has the drawback of removing items that may still be receiving some use from the most crowded sections and leaving the old, unused materials undisturbed in some other sections.[15]

How does a selector decide when something is sufficiently old to remove it from the reference collection? While some titles are obvious —a five-year-old telephone directory will have practically no value— others make for more difficult judgments. Many libraries buy several encyclopedias, updating one set each year over a three-, four-, or five-year cycle. That results in at least one of the sets being left in reference when it is several years old. Is this too out-of-date? In most print en-cyclopedias, only a small percentage of the articles are updated in each new annual edition. Most of what is printed in a five-year-old encyclo-pedia is still accurate. Another title with more current information can be used for population figures, news events of the past couple of years, and the like. Yet some users will still resort to that oldest encyclopedia and read facts that are outdated. Therefore, the newest available titles are always preferred for reference use. On the other hand, money spent on a new edition of the same encyclopedia every year is money that cannot be spent on other sources. Consequently, many libraries decide to use a rotating schedule to purchase these titles on a less fre-quent basis.[16] Methods to keep track of this schedule are described later in this book.

Sometimes a title is deemed to be outdated, but no new edition of it is available and no suitable replacement is found. Should this title re-main in reference? Again, judgment and consideration of the needs of the library's users are needed. If these users will be likely to pull erro-neous information out of this source and apply it to significant affairs (such as business plans or published articles), then the title should be weeded. However, sometimes the major use of a title is more as a demonstration or educational device, and the datedness of the source is less critical. For example, Trinity University often purchases the pre-vious edition of the *Simmons Study of Media & Markets,* which is much less expensive than purchasing the current edition. The source is used by communications and marketing students in mock marketing plans, teaching them how companies use consumer marketing data. No one is expected to use the volumes for current input into real business activities. Housing the set as a noncirculating title in the main stacks would be another option, of course, but the almost mandatory explanations the title requires make its location in reference more helpful to the students. Purchasing an outdated source such as this has a negligible effect on users and frees up funds for other sources that would otherwise go unpurchased.

Who Makes the Weeding Decisions?

Chapter 3 looked at the issues surrounding reference collection management and personnel. It is possible, however, that a different pattern may be needed for weeding from the collection. Once a title has been housed in the reference collection, adequate judgments about how much it has been used by librarians and patrons cannot be assessed by just one librarian, at least in most libraries with multiple reference staff. The original selector of the title may not be the most frequent user of that title. Hence, it can be helpful to have at least two people, and possibly a small committee, responsible for suggesting and making final weeding decisions so that multiple perspectives can be brought to bear on the sources. Within this group should be at least one person with substantial subject expertise in the area being weeded and another with substantial reference desk experience. Preferably, all of the members of the weeding team should have some reference service experience.

From this start, several different methods of using staff can be followed. At Trinity University the principal subject selector for a discipline (who is also a reference librarian) approves the weeding request forms for his or her weeded titles; then the head of reference must also initial the requests. In larger libraries where the head of the department is less involved in reference desk and selection work, this second person could be the coordinator of reference collection development. Other libraries have used teams of several librarians who divide up the subject areas, cull out sources, and place them in a central review area, then await comments from either the rest of the group or the entire reference staff. An important step followed by several libraries is requiring a person who disagrees with the weeding decision to justify that disagreement; otherwise, the source is weeded. This prevents the loss of momentum when any possible objection, however weak, causes the sources to be retained in the collection. Due to the general reluctance of many to weed, this more forceful approach seems warranted.

Implementation of Weeding

Success in weeding is most likely when weeding is integrated into the routine management of the reference collection. That is, sporadic episodes of weeding may remove unwanted materials, but the collection suffers from not having this done on a more regular and gradual basis. Reference selectors should work with their departments and their supervisors to institutionalize a systematic weeding effort that is performed regularly and routinely, rather than as shelving space crises arise. Routine weeding will also make the job more manageable, preventing the almost overwhelming task that comes from allowing the collection to be thoroughly overgrown.

The weeding program should attempt to cover the entire reference collection during an established span of time. This time will be determined by the size of the collection, available staff time, and how seriously overgrown that particular collection has become. For instance, Welch reports that the normal cycle at her university library is seven years.[17] Other libraries may decide that a considerably shorter time frame would serve best. It is conceivable that a program may acknowledge that some subject areas need more attention to cull the obsolete materials, such as medicine and health, and so implement faster review cycles for those subjects. In fact, if a library has done little weeding in the past and is just starting a new program, the time-sensitive areas that are most affected by obsolete information should be tackled first, for instance, medicine, law, science and technology, business, and statistics.

Of course, if weeding has not been done for some time, starting to remove the oldest material first is also useful. Majka created a database of all reference collection titles in a branch library, then produced lists sorted by subject and date.[18] Selectors were alerted to sources that appeared to be seriously outdated and were able to evaluate those sources quickly. Although this sort of database would be useful for virtually any library, considerable staff time went into its creation. Many online catalogs can provide at least some basic sorting by reference location and by date.

A title cannot be weeded in isolation; each source is a piece of the overall reference collection. When considering the withdrawal of a source, selectors should familiarize themselves with the other sources in that particular subject and determine whether a new edition or title should be ordered to replace the weeded item or whether the remainder of the collection contains recent sources that fill the same needs. The weeding process can be done by browsing the shelves and seeing what is presently on the shelves; although this might miss some titles that are in use on occasion, at least the missed titles are the ones in use and therefore less likely to need to be weeded. On the other hand, reference collections suffer from theft and mislaid materials, so a shelflist inventory, matching each item in the library's database with what is found on the shelf, will help alert staff to missing volumes as well.

A decision will need to be made about the ultimate disposition of weeded items. Some items are still suitable for keeping in the circulating stacks because they might be useful for historical perspectives on the subject. Old volumes of periodical indexes may be seldom used, but most libraries hesitate to throw them away. Occasionally, a user or library staff member will need to verify an old citation, and these sources can come in handy. Some materials may be useful in other, less-critical locations than the main reference collection. A common practice is sending the second most recent edition of a title to a branch library, another reference desk in the same building, or perhaps to a library or campus office that could still make use of a somewhat outdated source. Other materials may have a fairly short shelf life or have been worn out physically and are best sent directly to the trash bin. In some libraries, the same persons doing the weeding can make these decisions. Large libraries with subject selectors outside the reference department may want to have the subject selectors decide the ultimate disposition of these sources. Selectors should be cautious, however, of automatically consigning all weeded materials to the main collection because many old reference sources have minimal future utility.

Finally, systematic weeding projects should be coordinated with other library departments that will be affected by them. Cataloging staff will need to relocate or withdraw each item, and these items will be in addition to their normal workflow of new items. Unfortunate stories of a lack of cooperation between reference and cataloging units, and the resultant inability of reference staff to remove unwanted items from their collections, have been told at library conferences. It is vital that reference staff understand what sort of work load cataloging staff can handle, and procedures should be worked out to make sure decisions are clearly documented and approved. This situation makes another strong argument for systematic weeding, for it should be much easier for other departments to anticipate and plan for weeded materials as a regular stream, rather than infrequent deluges of books. Circulation staff also are often affected by weeding because they will need to find room in the stacks for the items relocated to the circulating collections. Large numbers of volumes in any one call number area, especially multivolume sets or runs of serials, will often require books to be shifted in the stacks. Again, a steady stream works best for this problem. If a large series of volumes must be weeded at one time, advance notice to circulation staff can permit them to plan their shifting activities ahead of time.

In libraries where a considerable number of titles will be weeded, cataloging staff may prefer that the reference department not send the physical volumes to cataloging at the time of the weeding decisions. Perhaps an easier way to manage this process is to send only decision forms from the weeding participants to cataloging. Cataloging staff are then free to retrieve the items from the reference collection as their work load permits them to process the materials. Cataloging avoids having large stacks of volumes awaiting processing, and the materials are more easily found by library users until they are removed. Of course, if a volume is falling apart or contains dangerously outdated information, there should be procedures to take the source physically to the cataloging department.

Weeding takes a fair amount of time—perhaps more than originally selecting the same sources—and has an impact on staff throughout the library. It is very important that general weeding policies and procedures be documented and approved by the library's administration (including the governing board for public libraries). The complete approval of a weeding program by those to whom the librarians ultimately report provides protection for the staff in case of challenges from those who are intrinsically opposed to weeding, provides institutional motivation for performing the tasks regularly, and provides an agreed-upon framework for interdepartmental cooperation.

Location

Much of the discussion in this and other chapters has referred mostly to "the reference collection." Of course, this is merely a way of giving a handle to the entire range and location of sources used for reference services in libraries. Virtually no library of any size today has its reference sources located in just one call number sequence in one shelving area. Large libraries may have multiple reference desks or branches. Increasingly, the movement toward electronic reference sources means that much of the collection is actually accessed remotely, outside the library. There is little doubt that this trend will continue, though the expense of having all indexes and encyclopedias, for example, online and networked will be prohibitive for most libraries. Reference departments that want to provide the best possible resources will still be purchasing printed products along with the electronic, and so departments will still need to decide on how to arrange their physical volumes as well as their computer workstations.

There is no one best way to arrange the materials in a reference department. In quite small libraries, it is even conceivable that reference books can be interfiled with those in the circulating collection. As long as the reference staff is able to use them for patron assistance in that arrangement, this method makes sense. In most libraries, however, the size of the collection will necessitate at least the separation of the reference sources from the rest of the collection. Most libraries will also have several different sublocations in their reference areas: ready reference, atlas case, periodical indexes, encyclopedias, vertical file, national bibliographies, and so on.

Different locations in reference are logical for some sorts of materials. Atlases, because of their size, often will not fit easily in the normal shelf spacing for books, and the large ones require a large work area for viewing, thus making a separate atlas area useful. The same problem causes many libraries to shelve the large national bibliographies in a separate section. Periodical indexes are sometimes shelved sequentially by call number with other reference books and sometimes on separate index shelving, often to give larger work surfaces for users who need to peruse a number of these good-sized volumes. A number of libraries prefer to group indexes by related subjects, for instance, education and psychology titles, and place these together.

There is a trade-off for the convenience of locating some materials separately: users can frequently become lost trying to find them. As an example, at Trinity University's library, users can find materials with a call number beginning with E in the following locations: main stacks, folios, reference, U.S. documents, Texas documents, San Antonio documents, documents microfiche, special collections, browsing, reserve, and media department (and perhaps one or two additional places). Within the reference department, call numbers with E could be located in the main reference stacks, ready reference, atlases, or periodical indexes. Each of these locations is labeled in the online catalog and on the materials, but the possibility of confusion in the minds of users unfamiliar with the library should be noted by the reference staff.

The clustering of certain types of resources by subject or format within the reference collection can be convenient for the user who wishes to use a number of related sources, but librarians need to remember that many users will prefer to work on their own and will want to locate the sources on their own. Again, relying on experience and anecdotal evidence, librarians see more confusion in finding sources as the number of sublocations expands. Consequently, collections with several sublocations should take steps to prevent as much confusion as possible. Certainly the locations should be accurately listed in the catalog, and charts or other visual aids should clearly indicate where each sublocation is found. Since many users will see a designation for "reference" in the catalog and ignore a more specific location, it can be very helpful to put some type of indicator in the main reference stacks telling where the items pulled out of the sequence are now located. Book dummies (wood or plastic blocks with a notation of the title and call number for a relocated item) can be placed in the stacks where the items would have been, had they not been moved to a sublocation. The problem with book dummies is that the lightweight ones fall off the shelves easily, and the heavier wooden ones can be both expensive and dangerous to unsuspecting heads. Another alternative is placing some sort of sign in the main reference stacks with a pointer to the new location. However, this cannot easily be done for large numbers of titles, so it is perhaps best reserved for the most heavily used titles.

Librarians tend to have strong feelings for or against the idea of creating separate reference desks and collections for various subjects. Many large public libraries have a business and economics reference collection, one for the sciences, and so on. Large academic library systems often have many branch subject libraries, and others have multiple reference areas within the same building. The obvious concern here is whether the improvement in the concentration of specialists and collections offsets the greater breadth that comes from offering library users reference service from one central location. Another concern is the possible duplication of sources that multiple reference collections require. Some of the basic reference sources are valuable for inquiries in many subject areas, and selectors will then have to decide whether they can afford to buy copies of them for more than one library. Reference collection management in this sort of environment requires that selectors remain aware of what is being added to each of the different reference collections, attempt to minimize unnecessary duplication of purchases, and find ways to share information quickly and efficiently with the users who need reference service at other library locations.

One location question that has been a bit problematic for many libraries is the location of subject bibliographies. Both the Library of Congress and the Dewey Decimal classification schemes allow subject bibliographies to be classified in the bibliography range of numbers (the Zs for LC; *010* and following numbers for DDC). It is a Library of Congress practice to provide classification numbers in both the bibliography range and in the subject range, although LC shelves its own holdings in the Zs. So, for example, bibliographies in religion may be shelved in the Z range, rather than in the *BL-BX* range. In a Library of Congress survey about the usefulness of the alternative, subject-based call numbers, LC found that more than two-thirds of respondents said that they use the subject, rather than bibliography, numbers.[19] Users are probably best served by locating all but the most general bibliographies in their subject areas, where they can browse bibliographies along with subject encyclopedias and dictionaries. One exception that makes sense for users appears to be the class numbers for author bibliographies in the LC system. LC classification of authors is notoriously hard to browse, but author bibliographies in the Z8000 and up range file neatly by authors' names, making this an easy section to browse.

Routine Maintenance

The addition of new volumes to a reference collection requires that staff be alert to any earlier editions or volumes that should be relocated. Staff should also be aware of times when paperbound issues of reference serials need to be sent to a bindery and should perform this service in ways that minimize disruptions to a library's users.

Adding New Books

The addition of new books to the reference collection offers the opportunity to stay aware of any other changes that should be made at the same time. In particular, checks should be made of whether an earlier edition of the same work is already in the collection. The person shelving the new titles should be on the lookout for this, which might recommend using trained staff rather than student workers or volunteers for the original shelving of new titles. When an older edition is located, some form of notification should be sent to the reference collection coordinator, who can then make a determination about relocating the older volume. Better yet is setting up a procedure in which cataloging staff routinely catch the new edition during processing and ask for relocation or withdrawal instructions from reference staff. A form inserted in the book with a request for instructions usually works quite well.

Adding New Serials Volumes

Reference serials make up a large share of the new items added to the collection. For some titles, such as periodical indexes, libraries may keep all or most of the entire run in the reference collection. For others, such as business annuals, perhaps the current year is the only one kept in reference. Reference selectors and cataloging staff need to have a predetermined retention pattern for serials. Major options include

> all issues including current and retrospective kept in reference, which can eventually create a serious space problem
>
> a certain number of current issues kept in reference, with earlier issues being relocated to the stacks or another location (for example, the current year only in reference)
>
> a certain number of current issues kept in reference, with earlier issues being discarded

Another option exists for reference serials that are not received regularly on subscription. Selectors may decide to purchase only occasional copies of a particular title, deciding that a new version every other year, or even less often, will still serve reference needs. However, when these titles are listed in the library's catalog, users and librarians alike can be confused about whether a volume from an earlier year is actually the most current; if there is another, more recent copy elsewhere; or if there is a problem with the subscription. The solution at Trinity University has been to label these titles "latest acquired edition only," rather than "latest edition only," thereby alerting users that the edition currently on the shelf may not be the latest one published—it is merely the latest one the library owns.

Binding

Many reference serials are updated with paperback issues. If the issues are not replaced with bound, cumulative volumes, most libraries will want to have the paper issues bound. Commercial bindery services do a fine job, but most have a several week turnaround time for processing. Since the information in these updates is usually among the most recent available in the library and access is not possible when the issues are at the bindery, staff should schedule binding when it is the least inconvenient for their users. The schedule should be determined in consultation between the reference department and the technical services staff who may prepare the bindery shipments. Reference staff are aware of the use patterns for particular types of reference sources and can suggest when the best times would be for sending them out of the library. For instance, in academic libraries, summers are usually preferable to late in the terms, when student demand for reference serials is highest. However, faculty demands on materials can occur during the slow periods for students, when faculty have more time for their research. Knowing which academic departments are likely to have major research projects or assignments going at a certain time of the year can help determine the best scheduling. Public libraries have more variety in their usage levels, since much of their business is unrelated to the school year. Of course, K–12 school assignments have an impact on public libraries, so sources most used by children may again be best put off until summer or very early in academic terms. No theoretical schedule can easily accommodate most libraries; each one will make a determination based on its perceptions of heaviest patron demands.

No matter how low the usage usually is at any time of the year, some users will be inconvenienced by items sent out to a bindery. Reference selectors can minimize this somewhat. If multiple titles in a subject area, for example, two periodical indexes in business and economics, require binding of current issues, their binding schedules can be staggered to avoid having a number of the related titles out of the building at the same time. If available, online access to databases that are not normally under subscription may be used to substitute for the missing print issues; that is, perhaps a search of the same database or a related title on DIALOG or OCLC FirstSearch would take the place of the issues sent to the bindery.

Notes

1. A good recent overview is Susan C. Flood, *Guide to Managing Approval Plans* (Chicago: American Library Association, 1998).

2. For an example of a list of a large number of book vendors that offer approval plans as well as direct orders, see the excellent University of Washington Libraries Acquisitions Division Web page, online, available http://weber.u.washington.edu/~acqdiv/ (13 Apr. 1998).

3. The University of Washington site in note 2 includes its list of publishers that do not appear in any of its approval plans. See University of Washington Libraries Acquisitions Division, *Customer Must Order Direct Publishers,* 29 Sept. 1997, online, available http://weber.u.washington.edu/~acqdiv/cmod.html (13 Apr. 1998).

4. Mary Biggs, "Discovering How Information Seekers Seek: Methods of Measuring Reference Collection Use," in *Weeding and Maintenance of Reference Collections,* ed. Sydney J. Pierce (New York: Haworth, 1990), pp. 108–13; also published as *The Reference Librarian,* no. 29 (1990): 108–13.

5. The most recent RUSA Awards prior to this book's publication were listed in the "1997 RUSA Awards," *Reference & User Services Quarterly* 37 (fall 1997): 35. Prior awards can be found in *The Bowker Annual* (New York: R. R. Bowker) and some online booksellers, such as Amazon.com, online, available http://www.amazon.com (15 Apr. 1998).

6. Richard L. Hopkins, "Ranking the Reference Books: Methodologies for Identifying 'Key' Reference Sources," in *Opportunities for Reference Services: The Bright Side of Reference Services in the 1990's,* ed. Bill

Katz (New York: Haworth, 1991), pp. 77–102; also published as *The Reference Librarian*, no. 33 (1991): 77–102.

7. One such product is the *OCLC/AMIGOS Collection Analysis CD* (Dublin, Ohio: OCLC, various years), which is produced by OCLC and the AMIGOS regional library network; see a description at the AMIGOS Web site; available http://www.amigos.org/cacd.html (9 Apr. 1998).

8. Biggs, "Discovering How Information Seekers Seek," pp. 105–14.

9. Eugene A. Engeldinger, " 'Use' as a Criterion for the Weeding of Reference Collections: A Review and Case Study," in Pierce, *Weeding and Maintenance*, pp. 119–28; Karen A. Sendi, "Assessing the Functionality of the Reference Collection," *Collection Building* 15, no. 3 (1996): 17–21.

10. Christopher W. Nolan, "The Lean Reference Collection: Improving Functionality through Selection and Weeding," *College & Research Libraries* 52 (Jan. 1991): 86; Engeldinger, " 'Use' as a Criterion," p. 127.

11. Jeanie M. Welch, Lynn A. Cauble, and Lara B. Little, "Automated Reshelving Statistics as a Tool in Reference Collection Management," *RSR: Reference Services Review* 25, no. 3–4 (1997): 79–85.

12. Biggs, "Discovering How Information Seekers Seek," p. 114.

13. Stanley J. Slote, *Weeding Library Collections: Library Weeding Methods,* 4th ed. (Englewood, Colo.: Libraries Unlimited, 1997), pp. 5–6.

14. David R. Majka, "An Electronic Tickler File for Reference Collection Management," *Library Software Review* 14 (fall 1995): 147.

15. Engeldinger, " 'Use' as a Criterion," p. 121.

16. For examples of purchase schedules for reference titles, see this book's annotated bibliography for titles by Margaret Irby Nichols as well as Lynn Westbrook, "Weeding Reference Serials," *The Serials Librarian* 10 (summer 1986): 81–100, which gives specific guidelines for representative reference serials in many subject areas.

17. Welch, "Automated Reshelving Statistics," pp. 79–85.

18. Majka, "An Electronic Tickler File," pp. 146–53.

19. "The Use of Alternative Classification Numbers," *Cataloging Service Bulletin* no. 59 (winter 1993): 70–1.

७ ७

Collection Management
for Lean Budgets

Reference books and serials continue to be produced in large numbers, while at the same time exciting, new electronic reference sources are being created. Reference selectors have a wide range of possibilities for adding new materials to the reference collection. However, library budgets have not generally fared well during the last decade. Those responsible for supplying the funding to libraries have frequently determined that library budgets cannot continue to grow above, or even at, the inflation rate; many libraries have been forced to cut their budgets. Even for those libraries with generally healthy budgets unaffected by decreases in funding, budgets have been hit hard by the rapid rise in serials prices over many years. Serials such as periodical indexes and directories make up a large portion of most reference expenditures. Consequently, many reference selectors have been forced to operate their collections on a much leaner basis than was true in the past. Cancellation of titles that were formerly considered important reference sources has been all too common.

Therefore, this chapter presents a number of suggestions for cutting costs for reference selectors. Some of these tips involve trading off some preferred reference situations, such as having some duplication or the most recent editions of all works, against the realities of too little funding to carry out all that a selector might want to do. Selectors should review their collection emphases, which should be documented in their collection policies, and determine which aspects of their reference services can be trimmed back with the least effect on their primary clientele. For instance, it may be that sources usually used by K–12 students for class homework need not be quite as current as sources used by local business people for their management decisions, and thus more emphasis would be put on the business sources. These determinations will have to be made on the local level by selectors who know their collections and their clientele.

General Guidelines

As a general rule, selectors should avoid duplication of sources in the reference collection. Selectors tend to purchase many of the new reference books from reputable publishers, even when there are sources with similar coverage and quality already in the collection. Although nuances of treatment and coverage between two similar sources may make owning both of them desirable, this duplication should be considered in light of available funding. This holds true for exact duplication of sources as well. Many locations with multiple libraries, such as a university campus, often duplicate sources among the various branch libraries. For example, most of the branches might find the *Encyclopedia of Associations,* a general tool, valuable for their patrons. However, libraries that must look carefully at cost containment may have a hard time justifying this much duplication. For a ready-reference tool such as this, an alternative might be to have branch librarians call the one branch owning the source when a user needs some information from it.

Reliance on other libraries also begins to take on more importance as budgets become tighter. Selectors may commonly acquire some sources that fall outside the main scope of the library's collections; for instance, an academic library might provide reference books on recreational activities for its students. When looking to trim purchases, the selectors at the academic library may determine that this particular subject area is perhaps better provided by the local public library and thus eliminate these materials from future purchases. Referrals to other area libraries work best when they are for areas of secondary, not primary, importance for the local institution. However, small libraries with very limited budgets may be forced to rely heavily on other libraries even for some of their core reference needs.

Sharing resources with other libraries can also provide some budgetary relief. In locations where several libraries are in reasonably close proximity to each other, selectors at these different libraries may decide that one expensive reference source will be maintained by one library and other similarly expensive titles will be held by others. Arrangements to share the information among the various libraries' users can then include steps such as providing onsite access for the patrons, interlibrary lending, telephone reference assistance to the other libraries, or even faxing pages from one library to another. The major drawback to this situation, of course, is that a library's own users will usually want the information there and then, and unless the information can be speedily provided from another library, the users may be unsatisfied with any substantial delays.

Groups of libraries can often negotiate cheaper prices on the materials that they purchase. Selectors should always check to see whether any consortium memberships might give them discounts on subscriptions; these are especially common with electronic subscriptions. Many U.S. libraries belong to regional library networks, such as AMIGOS and SOLINET, which work with information providers to offer discounts to their member libraries. Books may also be acquired more cheaply through groups as well; some approval vendors and book jobbers give higher discounts to groups of libraries that together have a significant volume of purchases.

Cost sharing may also be pursued with some portion of the library's users. This is occasionally done in academic libraries when a particular department would like the library to obtain a source that the library staff have not been able to afford. The requesting department may be willing to put up some percentage of the cost, assuming that the library will pick up the remainder and provide access to and service for the reference source. Of course, if the source is extremely valuable for a significant number of the library's users, selectors should pursue methods of incorporating its purchase into the normal budget. However, when funds are previously allocated and the academic department's desire to purchase is strong, cost sharing can stretch the budget a little more.

Selectors should not pass up free sources of reference information that can be acquired. Governmental agencies at all levels often supply sources at low costs or for free; many of these items are statistical sources that are heavily requested in libraries. Reference selectors should also be wary of commercial publishers who take free government information, repackage it, and sell it for a substantial price. In some situations, the commercial publishers have provided a service by adding further value to the government's publications, but in other cases the only major differences are the names on the title page and the prices the library pays. Some commercial publishers have been willing to supply certain types of libraries with free copies of selected works; for example, World Book, Inc., has frequently supplied free copies of its encyclopedia to academic libraries with curriculum collections for teacher training.

A final general suggestion for watching the reference budget closely is to diminish the number of reference titles that are purchased sight unseen. Most libraries order some publications based on the titles or the subjects, but then they find the sources less useful than originally thought. Approval plans provide one method of avoiding this waste of funds; book reviews are another. Unfortunately, reviews of books and electronic products are often slow to be published, so selectors who wait for reviews must often delay their purchases of the newest titles.

Cost Savings for Reference Books

Many of the books purchased by libraries are not acquired directly from the publishers but from book jobbers or vendors. This usually results in savings not only on paperwork and processing but also on the prices paid for the books. Vendors purchase large quantities of materials from publishers and are able to receive a significant discount from them. Some of this discount is passed along to libraries. Vendor discounts vary according to the particular vendor and the discount that a library can negotiate. Some libraries find it profitable to track vendor discounts and performance, thereby using the most cost-effective source for each order.[1]

Reference titles are often expensive and therefore somewhat more difficult for publishers to sell than cheaper trade titles. To enhance sales, publishers will often run prepublication sales on these titles, taking 10 to 20 percent or more off the list prices of these titles. Consistently taking advantage of these sales can save libraries a considerable sum during any given year. Occasionally, a book vendor will offer the same (or even a larger) discount than the publisher, so it can pay to check with one's principal vendors before ordering directly from the publisher. The down side to ordering through prepublication sales is that the volumes are acquired before books have been through an approval process or been reviewed in the library press, so this method is safest when used for materials that appear to be obvious selections.

Selectors can also save money by purchasing less expensive versions of reference books. Some reference books can be purchased in paperback editions at a substantial discount from the clothbound editions.[2] Of course, paperback versions will not hold up as well to heavy use, and items selected for the reference collection are presumed to be sources with a fair amount of use. One way of dealing with this problem is to purchase paperback versions for titles whose older volumes are discarded and are replaced on a regular basis. For example, Trinity University's library purchases the college guides series from Peterson's in paperback each year because the library does not archive the older editions. However, some libraries find their budgets restricted enough to warrant purchasing paperback editions whenever possible. They may take a middle course and have their own library bindings put on these sources immediately after they are purchased; frequently, the cost of this process will be less than the cost difference between the publishers' cloth and paperbound versions.

Some of the larger, more expensive reference books are also produced in more-concise versions. For instance, Macmillan, one of the major reference publishers, previously produced the award-winning, but expensive, multivolume sets titled the *Encyclopedia of Religion* and the *Encyclopedia of Bioethics.* These sets currently retail for about $750 and $500. Macmillan also published concise, one-volume excerpts from these sets called *World Religions* and *Bioethics,* which sell for approximately $125 each. Although the coverage is obviously more limited, small libraries without the need for as much scholarly detail may find these alternatives more appealing than sets that they could never afford. Macmillan obviously believes that there is an untapped market for these less expensive versions.

Related to the idea of purchasing concise versions is the acquisition of subsets of some reference sets. McGraw-Hill, for example, has routinely published subsets of its large *Encyclopedia of Science and Technology* (retailing for nearly $2,000) to appeal to those libraries that want to purchase reference material for just one scientific discipline. Thus some libraries may find it more useful to purchase only the smaller encyclopedias dealing with chemistry, engineering, and environmental science, for example (each costing about $100). A university may purchase the large, comprehensive set for the main library and purchase the smaller sets for the branch libraries with special collections in those areas. However, libraries that are watching their budgets should be careful of purchasing the subsets in addition to the comprehensive set, unless that duplication is justified. Many unwary selectors may not realize that the subsets are just that and not new, independent publications—though occasionally a small amount of new material is added. When all of the different subsets are required, it can be more economical to buy only the major set.

Certain reference sources have multiple parts, all of which do not have the same usefulness. For example, Gale Research puts out regular editions of an excellent reference tool, the *Acronyms, Initialisms & Abbreviations Dictionary*, which defines the meaning of thousands of these cryptic items. Although it is expensive, many libraries own this and use it heavily. A more debatable purchase is the separately priced *Reverse Acronyms, Initialisms & Abbreviations Dictionary* that many libraries appear to order automatically along with the former title. The *Reverse* allows one to look up a word or group of words and find its abbreviation or acronym. Although this could be useful once in a while, the reverse process is not normally a heavy-demand item for reference desks. Selectors who purchase the volumes they are most interested in and avoid the less-needed volumes will save themselves some book money each year.

Another unnecessary purchase for many reference collections is a subject bibliography that is compiled from a readily available periodical index, for example, the ATLA Bibliography Series, which is taken from the *ATLA Religion Database*. If the library does not subscribe to the index, the bibliography may be a justifiable purchase. On the other hand, when the index is easily available to users, selectors need to decide if the value added to the citations by the compiler warrants spending money on citations that can be retrieved from the original database. This is not meant to disparage the bibliographies, which may be useful in many situations, but merely points out possible duplication that may not be obvious.

Many selectors save budget funds by alternating the purchases of similar types of resources in different years. This is most commonly done with encyclopedias, for which there are several worthy choices. Many selectors will buy, say, the *Encyclopaedia Britannica* one year, the *Encyclopedia Americana* the next year, *Collier's Encyclopedia* the third year, and then perhaps go back to the *Britannica* in the fourth year, and so on. This keeps at least one new encyclopedia edition in the collection at all times, while still providing different sources with their slightly different perspectives and coverage. This same pattern might be used in small libraries for other expensive purchases, such as world atlases. One disadvantage, of course, is that some users will end up using the oldest of the sources and stumbling upon the portion of them that is outdated.

The situation with encyclopedias has changed for many libraries because of their online availability. It is quite attractive to access *Britannica* or *Americana* through the Web and enjoy the most current revisions at any moment. However, selectors will not find the same alternating or rotating schedule to work with the online sources; once the subscription to an online source is canceled, users no longer have access. Therefore, libraries are more likely to continue to subscribe to the same online encyclopedia year after year. This takes funds away from the budget that could have been spent on new editions of the other encyclopedias. Thus librarians end up either spending more of their reference budgets on encyclopedias or diminishing the number of options they provide.

Finally, libraries with quite limited funds may be able to find occasional sources "previously owned." Some libraries are willing to pass along the next-to-the-last edition of a work that they have replaced; this is frequently done in the multilibrary situations of academic campuses and public libraries. The most current edition can be kept in the library with the most need for it, while a previous edition may suit most purposes that come up less frequently at a branch library. Used bookstores are occasionally options for finding used reference books, but this is less likely than finding more general books for the circulating collection because the sellers of used books—mainly individuals—are less likely to buy and quickly sell reference sources. Reference selectors adding used volumes to their collections must pay careful attention to how dated the information in these sources is; adding misleading or erroneous information to the reference collection in the cause of saving money is not a wise move. Unless the older volumes maintain a high degree of appropriateness for current use, they probably should be avoided. Contrary to some popular views, no information is often better than partially correct information.

Cost Savings for Reference Serials

Many of the most useful reference tools are serials, and their prices have been climbing along with the prices of other serials. As with a library's periodical list, the reference list of serials must be monitored closely. A regular review of the prices of titles and how much they have increased from the previous year helps maintain a sense of how much value the libraries receive for the expenditures. One way to approach this annual review is to look for titles that have increased the most in price, both by absolute cost and by percentage of increase.[3] Some producers of reference sources have raised their prices significantly more than their competitors, and selectors who believe that these price hikes are unreasonable may want to consider such titles as the ones to cancel first. Even if the raised prices are reasonable in terms of percentages, the absolute cost may be sufficient to place some titles at the front of the cancellation candidates.

Selectors looking for savings should carefully look for portions of reference serials that may not be needed, for example, encyclopedia yearbooks. This concept of not purchasing every update that is available is also a possibility for other reference serials. Some annual directories come with semiannual update volumes, often for a considerable price. Are enough changes made in the directories to require the midyear updates? Many of these could be canceled. Somewhat more radical would be canceling the updates to reference indexes in cases where timeliness is not as important or when updates are available through another channel. For instance, the excellent *CIS Index to Publications of the United States Congress* includes both monthly updates and a bound annual cumulation. Used to track recent legislative events, the *CIS Index* in its printed form is less up-to-date than free legislative sources available on the Internet. Selectors may want to maintain the acquisition and retention of the annual cumulations due to the fine archival history they provide, but cost savings could be obtained by canceling the print monthly issues and relying on a combination of the Internet and the bound cumulations, which can be purchased separately. This may not appeal to many selectors, but it could be workable and economical if it were necessary for their budgets.

Cumulations of multiple years of index volumes have been offered by several publishers over the years, notably for the Institute for Scientific Information's citation indexes, CIS's legislative and statistical sources, and *Chemical Abstracts.* These titles are all very costly and important in their fields. The amount of literature reviewed in any one year is large for these sources, so the idea of consolidating multiple years into cumulative volumes is logical. Researchers do not need to look through as many volumes (or discs, if using a CD-ROM version) when there are cumulations, and librarians may save some shelf space by removing the annuals. However, the price of this convenience is high; cumulations for these products can cost several thousands of dollars. When budgets are adequate, these cumulations provide a nice service to the library users. When budgets are tight, justifying their purchase may be somewhat more difficult for reference selectors, especially when they understand the amount of other reference sources they could purchase with the same funds.

Selectors may just avoid starting a subscription to a reference serial because they do not see the necessity of getting every updated volume. Instead, they may decide to purchase a serial volume as they would a monograph, acquiring a new one every few years, much as they do for encyclopedias that are in a rotation arrangement. Assuming the sources hold their reference value over these years, this method can produce a fair amount of savings. The difficulty with the method is keeping track of the items that need to be reordered at given intervals. If the sources are not on subscription or standing order, selectors may easily forget to purchase the new editions when the time is right. This problem also occurs with some reference tools that are published frequently but irregularly, so that librarians cannot be sure when they should order the newest version. These titles are "pseudoserials," since their frequency mimics that of serials, but they are not titles to which subscriptions can be entered. For example, Trinity University's library has this problem with the local chamber of commerce publications in San Antonio. The library would like to purchase each new update to these publications, but they are not always published at the same time; no subscription or standing order is possible. Carter gives a useful list of several types of problematic reference serials: highly irregular titles, titles that cannot be placed on standing order due to publisher restrictions, new titles lacking proof of their usefulness, small or local publishers' titles, and frequently revised monographs.[4]

One method to deal with pseudoserials and other reference materials ordered at irregular intervals is to create a tickler file, a list of sources and the times when they should be reordered. If the number of titles is not too large, a manual card file, arranged by date of reorder, should work fairly easily. For larger numbers of titles, use software to track the titles. The library at Trinity University uses a tickler file originally created in dBASE database software but now managed with a spreadsheet program (Microsoft Excel). As shown in figure 3, the file consists of titles, publishers, costs, intervals for purchasing, and the last and next dates for purchase. The advantage of the computer-based file is its ability to sort and retrieve any data. This file can be sorted by title, costs, and so on. Sorting by the next purchase date allows a selector to see which titles need to be ordered during a given budget year and approximately how much those titles will cost. This provides some prediction for upcoming costs, and selectors can spread out these costs among the different budget years in the cycle.

In addition to the approach shown in figure 3, other automated methods can track these problematic titles. Carter and colleagues used the INNOPAC integrated library system, creating special order records for those titles that fell into the problematic serial category. Regular reports were then forwarded to the coordinator of the reference collection, who recommended titles that needed to be reordered.[5] Majka created an electronic tickler file using FileMaker Pro database management software, in which he added every title from the reference collection of his branch library. Using a "tickler date" field, reports were generated that listed titles needing review for possible purchase at any given time.[6] The database also served as a basis for collection evaluation and weeding.

Some reference serials are now less expensive in electronic form than in paper. However, this is not always true; many publishers charge a premium for the digital version. Nevertheless, major savings are possible by switching some titles to the electronic versions and canceling

Figure 3. *Reference Serials/Pseudoserials Tickler File*

Title	Publisher	Call No.	Latest Owned	Price	Purch. Req. (yrs.)	Retention	Last Purch.	Next Purch.
Academic American Encyclopedia	Grolier	AE 5 A23	1995	500.00	4	Latest Ed Only	4/1/95	4/1/99
Accreditation Manual for Hospitals	Joint Commission on Accred.	RA 971 J55	1998	75.00	1	Earlier Eds Stacks	10/1/98	10/1/99
Acronyms, Initialisms, & Abbreviations Dictionary	Gale	PE 1693 G33	1997	575.00	3	Latest Acq Ed Only	1/1/97	1/1/00
Admission Requirements of U.S. & Canadian Dental Schools	Amer. Assn. Dental School	RK 91 A582	1996	20.00	3	Latest Acq Ed Only	10/1/96	10/1/99
American Medical Directory	American Medical Assoc.	R 15 A4385	1995	495.00	5	Latest Acq Ed Only	1/1/95	10/1/00
Annual Register of Grant Support	National Register	AS 911 A2 A67	1996	199.95	3	Latest Ed Only	1/1/97	1/1/00
Artist's Market	Writer's Digest	N 8600 A75 1988	1995	23.95	5	Earlier Eds Stacks	1/1/95	1/1/00
Best's Key Rating Guide: Property/Casualty	Best	HG 9765 B4	1997	95.00	3	Earlier Eds Stacks	2/1/97	2/1/00
Biography & Genealogy Master Index cumulative	Gale	CT 214 X2 B572	1995	925.00	5	All in Ref (cumulat.)	3/1/95	3/1/00
Business Rankings Annual	Gale	HG 4061 X2	1995	170.00	3	Earlier Eds Stacks	1/1/96	1/1/99
Canadian Almanac and Directory	Gale	AY 414 C2	1997	129.95	5	Earlier Eds Stacks	1/1/97	1/1/02
College Blue Book	Macmillan	LA 226 C685	1997	195.00	3	Latest Acq Ed Only	3/15/98	3/15/01
Collier's Encyclopedia	Macmillan Educational	AE 5 C683	1998	900.00	4	Latest Ed Only	4/1/98	4/1/02
Commonwealth Universities Yearbook	Assn. of Commonwealth Univ.	L 915 C6	1995	235.00	5	Latest Acq Ed Only	10/1/95	10/1/00

the print editions. As was mentioned in chapter 5, however, selectors need to judge additional factors such as ease of use and the ownership/archiving of data issues before making a quick decision to cancel the print copy. For some products the combined electronic and print costs are only slightly more than that for either one alone; in these cases, librarians concerned about archiving and dependable access may opt to keep both versions, choosing user convenience over cost savings.[7]

Finally, libraries can also go the "hand-me-down" route with serials as well as monographs, receiving recent but not current issues of reference serials from other libraries. One scenario that has worked well at some libraries is having one library in a multilibrary system or campus keep the most current issues of one title, while another library keeps the most recent of a similar title. As each title is superseded by a new issue, the replaced issues are sent to the other library. Swapping titles allows some overlap in serials titles to be maintained, while only one of the subscriptions must be purchased for each of the libraries. This procedure can also be used to save funds on titles used mostly for staff purposes. A publisher's directory that is used heavily by acquisitions staff, for instance, might be set up so that the most current volume is kept in acquisitions and the second most recent is kept in the reference collection; the reverse arrangement could also be used. Of course, care again must be exercised to keep any material that is obviously outdated from being used in reference. The relative currency of the superseded issue that is sent to reference should be evaluated. Selectors should always prefer to have the most current issues in reference, but tight budgets can sometimes make this difficult.

Cost Savings for Electronic Reference Products

A logical first step in reining in the budget for electronic sources is to take advantage of all the free sources that are currently available. Although the hype concerning what can be found on the Internet is not completely accurate, certainly many authoritative sources on the Internet can be used for reference purposes. Foremost among these may be the publications of various governments, including U.S. federal, state, and some local political entities. An extensive amount of demographic, economic, and other statistical information is readily searchable through freely available Web sites. Some of the better sites, such as that for the U.S. Census Bureau, allow users to customize the types of data they wish to display and print or download. Other government agencies provide travel and health information that is reliable and current. Many states have well-designed Web sites that showcase information about their states' economies and attractions.

A variety of other information creators and providers have placed their contributions on the Web for others to use. Scientific and other professional associations frequently provide information about themselves that would usually be found only in print directories. Scholars in various fields have put some of their research on the Web, though finding appropriate sites can be difficult. Commercial businesses have made their presence known on the Web, and many of them provide online catalogs, recent financial information, and other information that would usually require purchasing some of the expensive business reference tools. Librarians and others have found a great amount of usefulness in online booksellers, such as Amazon.com and Barnes and Noble. Their online catalogs provide verification of titles and authors, ISBNs, dates of publication, and so on. They are normally more up-to-date than printed copies of sources like *Books in Print*. Of course, these sites may not have everything that a good business reference tool would supply, and the accuracy of the information must be evaluated, but they can be most useful for limited-budget libraries.

Internet resources seem to change daily, so it is quite difficult for selectors to stay abreast of available reference sources. Many librarians have created lists of these types of reference sources on their Web pages; most of them give pointers to major collections of online reference sources. Perhaps one of the best places to start looking for free Internet reference sources is at the Internet Public Library, an online service sponsored by the School of Information at the University of Michigan.[8] The IPL contains hundreds of pointers to directories, statistical sources, collections of biographical data, literary criticism, and more.

A tried-and-true method for saving reference expenditures has been the cancellation of print reference sources that may be searched through online vendors. This is especially useful for those reference tools that are expensive in print and not used on a regular and heavy basis. For instance, many libraries have canceled titles such as *Biological Abstracts* or *Chemical Abstracts*, which are among the most expensive indexes to which libraries subscribe. In the place of the print subscriptions, some libraries have offered subsidized or free online searches through DIALOG, Ovid, STN, or other online vendors. The online searches may be fairly expensive, but an analysis done before the format is switched can tell selectors whether the total cost to the library of performing the online searches will be cheaper than the print price. The analysis will need to consider the impact on reference staff, unless the online searching is set up for end users to search. Mediated searches can occupy a substantial amount of staff time. However, with the advent of Web-based searching methods, more and more databases are searchable by end users, and many libraries are seeing a decrease in the number of mediated searches they perform.

When libraries subscribe to electronic reference sources, there are ways to keep the costs down. Selectors should look at all options that affect the library's subscription price. The most notable of these options is the number of simultaneous users that will access the databases. CD-ROM subscriptions commonly cost one price for stand-alone installations where only one user at a time can access the product, sometimes a higher price for a networked version with just one simultaneous user, and higher rates for larger numbers of users. Some online vendors charge on this same model. Although the idea of having enough user licenses so that no user will ever need to wait is laudable, this is not realistic when the budget is being stretched too thin. Selectors should evaluate how often a product is used and how low the number of licenses could be without seriously impeding the work of their users. Care should be taken not to overestimate the number needed because of short periods of heavy use. For example, class assignments in schools or colleges can often create a strong demand for a product for one or two weeks; after that time, the product is only occasionally used. Selectors might need to keep the number of simultaneous users to a low figure, then speak with instructors and students to apprise them of this situation. Faculty can be encouraged to provide enough time for all students to get to the product, perhaps over an extended time.

Besides providing basic cost savings through a volume discount, consortial purchasing of online products can also help with the pricing problem of simultaneous users. When one considers that many products are used in the sporadic way described in the last paragraph, and that this sporadic use may come at different times at different libraries, then it is apparent that pooling the libraries' users together will tend to spread out the demand somewhat. Thus fewer simultaneous-user licenses may be needed for a consortium of libraries than would be required if each member library individually purchased enough licenses for its own users.

Of course, the best possible scenario would be to acquire electronic products that do not charge anything extra for networking or multiple user access. Several vendors offer their products at no extra charge for networks within the same building or, for some vendors, within the same local institution. Librarians who are carefully watching a small acquisitions budget for reference sources may decide that some of these products are better choices even if the content is not as substantial as that of the more expensive sources.

Many electronic products will never be used heavily enough to justify paying networking subscription fees, or for that matter investing in network hardware and software. These products will work fine as single-user sources. For online services, users generally need only a computer workstation and a communications line. Sources can be listed on workstation menus, and different potential users can compete for the one available connection. CD-ROM products are somewhat more difficult to manage, since the library must have both properly equipped workstations and a place to store the CDs when they are not in use. CD jukeboxes, which swap discs to a player as they are requested, are a high-tech solution, but one most budget-minded libraries will not wish to use. Instead, one option found workable at Trinity University is checking out each CD to use on reference workstations. Discs can be kept at the reference desk or stored at the circulation desk when the reference desk is closed. Individual discs can be monitored this way, and users share several multiproduct workstations.

An alternative to an online service subscription is transaction-based pricing. Unfortunately, doing so with the traditional online vendors, which charge per minute of connect-time and per citation displayed, can be dangerous—librarians have no way of knowing how much the service might be used and how high the next bill might be. One useful solution to this problem has been offered by OCLC's FirstSearch service.[9] Libraries may subscribe to many of the First-Search databases, but another option is to pay by the search. Each search statement entered by a user incurs a flat search charge, which is usually quite reasonable. No extra citation charges are made. Selectors can purchase a set number of searches ahead of their use, then allow users to use the databases until the prepaid searches run out. The big advantages to this sort of transaction-based pricing are that libraries pay for only the amount of searching done in a particular database and that a cap is put on the total amount of money spent on the service. Of course, if too few searches are purchased, a library may need to go back to the budget to pay for more searches or may need to turn off access to the databases until the next budget cycle. For libraries on limited budgets, librarians may need to monitor use of these prepaid searches carefully.

Finally, to repeat an earlier point: many of the electronic reference sources can be acquired less expensively by subscribing as part of a group of libraries, whether as a local consortium, part of a regional library network, or a newly created ad hoc group. Vendors are looking for ways to gain greater market share and economies of scale during this formative period for electronic resources, and libraries that can bargain as part of a group will almost always be able to achieve a lower cost than those that purchase on their own.

Notes

1. University of Washington Libraries, Acquisitions Division, *U.S. Vendor Discounts,* online, available http://weber.u.washington.edu/~acqdiv/vendisc.html/ (13 Apr. 1998).

2. Andrew L. March, ed., *Recommended Reference Books in Paperback,* 2d ed. (Englewood, Colo.: Libraries Unlimited, 1992).

3. Heather S. Miller, "Keeping the Lid On: Approaches to the Control of Costs in Reference Book Purchasing in an Academic Library," in *The Publishing and Review of Reference Sources,* eds. Bill Katz and Robin Kinder (New York: Haworth, 1987), pp. 281–302; also published as *The Reference Librarian,* no. 15 (1986): 281–302.

4. Christina E. Carter, Nina K. Stephenson, and Frances C. Wilkinson, "Putting the House in Order: Using INNOPAC to Manage Problematic Reference Serials and Pseudoserials," *RSR: Reference Services Review* 24 (spring 1996): 17.

5. Carter, "Putting the House in Order," pp. 18–20.

6. David R. Majka, "An Electronic Tickler File for Reference Collection Management," *Library Software Review* 14 (fall 1995): 146–53.

7. George S. Machovec, "The Retention of Print Sources in View of Electronic Databases," *Colorado Libraries* 16 (Sept. 1990): 27.

8. Internet Public Library, *Reference Center*, online, available http://www.ipl.org/ref/ (4 May 1998).

9. Read a description of FirstSearch at OCLC's Web site, available http://www.oclc.org (3 May 1998).

ɚ Selected Bibliography ᴌ

This bibliography includes those publications, print and electronic, that have been most useful in my work on reference collection management. This list is by no means comprehensive, but the titles include some of the best work that has been done on this topic. Note that there are some special categories of sources excluded from this bibliography: selection sources cited and annotated in chapter 4, general collection development texts that have only limited comments on reference collections, and articles that evaluate specific electronic titles. Only a small selection of the many recent publications on selection of electronic resources are included. The line between general electronic sources and reference sources has become fuzzy, even more so with the growth of the Internet. Included are a few publications on Internet resources that have a particular relevance to the provision of reference services.

American Library Association. *Principles for Licensing Electronic Resources.* Chicago: American Library Association, 1998. Online. Available http://www.ala.org/washoff/ip/license.html. 13 Apr. 1998.

> Recognizing the increasingly important place that license agreements occupy in library uses of electronic products, ALA brought together a working group of several library associations to create these principles. Legal background and definitions are provided, then fifteen principles are proposed. Aimed at library staff who accept or negotiate such licenses, the principles are intended to protect the ownership rights of publishers while still protecting the legal rights of libraries (including refusal of library responsibility for the misuse of a licensed product by a user).

Anderson, Byron. "Reference Works from Selected Small Alternative Presses." *RSR: Reference Services Review* 25 (summer 1997): 65–72.

Anderson contends that small and alternative presses publish materials that the increasingly centralized big publishers find too controversial or unlikely to sell in large numbers. Small presses provide voices for marginalized concerns. The article acquaints the reference selector with forty-three reference titles that have been produced by twenty-five alternative presses. Subjects vary, but most of the sources relate to information about minorities, women, and social change. All of the titles were published between 1992 and 1997 and were in print at the time the article was published. Anderson gives not only full bibliographical citations and brief annotations but also addresses, phone and fax numbers, and e-mail addresses or URLs for each small press.

Awe, Susan C. *ARBA Guide to Subject Encyclopedias and Dictionaries.* 2d ed. Englewood, Colo.: Libraries Unlimited, 1997.

Providing perhaps the most complete recent list of subject encyclopedias and dictionaries, this guide reprints the *American Reference Books Annual* reviews for these types of reference books that were published over a ten-year period. Titles no longer available are omitted, and those reviews that required new information have been updated. The reviews average approximately 250 words each, tend to include some critical evaluation along with the description, and cover popular as well as scholarly titles. Awe's guide is useful but not essential for libraries subscribing to *ARBA.*

Balay, Robert. "Notes from the Jurassic." *Against the Grain* 9 (Sept. 1997): 24, 26.

The editor of the *Guide to Reference Books* and the reference sources section of *Choice* describes the features that make great reference books. These include having a broad scope with big files, being rooted in traditional scholarship, providing a framework to the discipline a reference book covers, and covering all types of materials and formats within each subject area. His notes are interesting in that they run contrary to the direction of many publishers today that publish smaller, narrower types of reference sources. Note that this issue of *Against the Grain* is a "reference publishing issue" and contains many other interesting interviews and short articles.

Bates, Marcia J. "What is a Reference Book? A Theoretical and Empirical Analysis." *RQ* 26 (fall 1986): 37–57.

> Bates has a knack for making complex problems understandable and finding complexities in seemingly simple situations. In this article, she looks at the makeup of reference books and determines that their distinguishing feature is their organizational structure of ordered files and records—characteristics that make a reference book useful for consultation. She then analyzes materials in the collections of selected libraries and discovers that virtually all books shelved in reference collections are predominantly files and that most books shelved in the circulating stacks are mainly narrative text, thus supporting her theoretical definition.

Batt, Fred. "The Detailed Reference Collection Development Policy: Is It Worth the Effort?" In *Evaluation of Reference Services*, edited by Bill Katz and Ruth A. Fraley, 313–19. New York: Haworth, 1984. Also published as *The Reference Librarian*, no. 11 (1984): 313–19.

> Batt argues that extensive reference collection development policies are a waste of staff time. He notes that most colleagues he has asked about these policies admit that they seldom or never consider the policies' contents when going about their daily selection tasks. Batt does admit that some guidelines can be useful for beginning reference librarians, but he feels that a basic outline of possibly just one page could be as helpful as a larger policy document. Instead of using a policy for guiding selection and evaluation, the author argues that careful review of what works and what does not work during everyday reference activities will provide the guidance needed to keep the collection in top shape.

Berkeley Digital Library SunSITE. *Digital Library SunSITE Collection and Preservation Policy.* Berkeley, Calif.: University of California Libraries, June 6, 1996. Online. Available http://sunsite.berkeley.edu/admin/collection.html. 16 May 1998.

This online document, like the others linked to it, contains an excellent outline of the major methods in which electronic information can be collected: archived, in which the material is hosted locally and will be kept on a permanent basis; served, in which the material resides on a local machine but without a commitment for permanent archiving; mirrored, in which a copy of the material is hosted locally, but the local library makes no commitment for archiving and assumes the original host has responsibility for the content; and linked, in which the materials are hosted elsewhere and the library merely points to its location.

Biggs, Mary, and Victor Biggs. "Reference Collection Development in Academic Libraries: Report of a Survey." *RQ* 27 (fall 1987): 67–79.

This survey was an important factor in motivating librarians to look more carefully at the state of their reference collections. The authors discovered that most reference collections were too big to be used effectively, that written collection development policies were in place in few libraries, that weeding policies and the practice of weeding were even less common, and that most of the sources in reference collections are not used during any particular year.

Boon, Belinda. *The CREW Method: Expanded Guidelines for Collection Evaluation and Weeding for Small and Medium-Sized Public Libraries.* Revised and updated ed. Austin, Texas: Texas State Library, 1995.

An excellent primer for weeding smaller collections, the *CREW Method* emphasizes the importance of Continuous Review, Evaluation, and Weeding. Reasons for weeding collections and responding to antiweeding sentiment are explained cogently. A short section on reference weeding gives suggested guidelines for retention of major reference formats such as almanacs and directories. Additional suggestions are provided for the entire collection according to Dewey class numbers.

Bopp, Richard E., and Linda C. Smith, eds. *Reference and Information Services: An Introduction.* 2d ed. Englewood, Colo.: Libraries Unlimited, 1995.

Bopp and Smith currently edit one of the best reference services textbooks on the market. The volume contains chapters by the editors as well as several selected contributors. The first half of the book reviews major issues in reference librarianship, such as the reference interview, trends in electronic resources, library instruction, and management and evaluation activities. The second half provides an outline of major reference sources by type, such as encyclopedias and biographical sources. Each of these latter chapters describes the criteria used to evaluate such sources, then provides a bibliographical essay that introduces students to the major works. In addition to the usual bibliographic references, annotated reading lists are provided for all chapters.

Boyarski, Jennie S. "Harnessing CD-ROMs and Collection Policies." In *Community College Reference Services*, edited by Bill Katz, 160–6. Metuchen, N.J.: Scarecrow, 1992.

Selection of electronic formats should be integrated into normal collection development activities, Boyarski states, and she believes that selectors need to gain the skills to be competent evaluators of software and hardware. She also believes that criteria tailored for the digital sources are required, and she provides a checklist for selecting CD-ROM resources.

Carter, Christina E., Nina K. Stephenson, and Frances C. Wilkinson. "Putting the House in Order: Using INNOPAC to Manage Problematic Reference Serials and Pseudoserials." *RSR: Reference Services Review* 24 (spring 1996): 13–20, 72.

The authors give a fine overview of the problems that serials and serial-like monographs can cause acquisitions and reference staff, thus leading to missed issues and forgotten reorders. An especially clear treatment of pseudoserials is given, pointing out how some sources are revised regularly but cannot be acquired via subscription.

Clark, Juleigh Muirhead, and Karen Cary. "An Approach to the Evaluation of Ready Reference Collections." *RSR: Reference Services Review* 23 (spring 1995): 39–44.

Reporting on a project completed at Virginia Commonwealth University in 1991, the authors describe the overly large ready reference collection that they felt needed to be reduced greatly in size. Many of the titles were rarely used. By sending all of these titles to the regular reference stacks, and then returning only those that met the new ready reference criteria, a section of more than 200 titles was reduced to a functional 34 titles. The authors make good points about the advantages of a small ready reference collection.

Coleman, Kathleen, and Pauline Dickinson. "Drafting a Reference Collection Policy." *College & Research Libraries* 38 (May 1977): 227–33.

One of the earliest articles to call for the development of a separate reference collection policy, this piece outlines some features that should be included in every document. Then it presents the San Diego State University policy as a detailed example.

Collection Development & Evaluation Section, Reference and User Services Association, American Library Association. *Collection Development Policies Committee.* Online. Available http://academic.uofs. edu/organization/codes. 11 May 1998.

This ALA committee is attempting to collect and analyze collection development policy statements for electronic formats. An archive of such statements has been physically deposited with ALA, but this Web site provides links to the text of a number of policies as well as an annotated bibliography and a "core policy elements" document.

Crawford, Walt, and Michael Gorman. *Future Libraries: Dreams, Madness, and Reality.* Chicago: American Library Association, 1995.

Written as an antidote to the calls for a virtual library, this small volume presents a compelling argument for the future of libraries as one with books *and* the Web, printed journals *and* electronic serials. The authors incisively discuss which information technologies work well in electronic formats (periodical indexes, union catalogs, etc.) and which perform better in their print versions (lengthy expositions, for example). Excessive claims of those driven by "technolust" are debunked, and the proponents of an all-virtual library are seen as intentional or unintentional enemies of libraries. The authors call for gradual implementation of electronic resources where they make economic and ergonomic sense, while retaining the use of print for its proven suitability for many tasks.

Demas, Samuel. "Collection Development for the Electronic Library: A Conceptual and Organizational Model." *Library Hi Tech* 12, no. 4 (1994): 71–80.

Demas provides a systematic discussion of the need for subsuming all library collecting efforts into one collection development policy. He discusses the impact of electronic sources on library collection development staff and posits a number of "information genres" with which the selectors must become knowledgeable. Several decision-assisting forms are appended to the article.

Demas, Samuel, Peter McDonald, and Gregory Lawrence. "The Internet and Collection Development: Mainstreaming Selection of Internet Resources." *Library Resources & Technical Services* 39 (July 1995): 275–90.

Demas and colleagues, all from Cornell University libraries, report on their growing effort to incorporate Internet resources seamlessly into the libraries' collections. Participating selectors began to locate appropriate Internet resources for their own collections and decided how best these could be treated. An assumption of the project was that adding specific titles, rather than pointing to collections of resources or pointers on other servers, would best benefit their libraries. In systematic fashion, the bibliographers located and discussed more than 1,000 potential sites, created a taxonomy of Internet resources, and began writing a collection policy that would include criteria and selecting intensity for each taxonomic category. Several selectors were assigned the role of becoming experts within certain categories for all formats, giving them the ability to consider the best formats for their libraries. This necessitated both additional staff training, so that selectors would be competent to search and evaluate the Internet, and upgraded selectors' workstations, so that they could handle any of the new media displays and downloads. The authors append helpful lists of their access tiers, a taxonomy of Internet resources, and an excerpt from their collection policy. Overall, this is one of the best discussions of how libraries can deal with Internet resources.

Dickinson, Gale K. *Selection and Evaluation of Electronic Resources.* Englewood, Colo.: Libraries Unlimited, 1994.

Dickinson covers the types of electronic sources currently available—full-text, bibliographic, numeric, and directory—and provides methods for evaluating how well these sources fit into a library's collection. She pays close attention to practical issues, such as printing, use of stand-alone workstations for CD products, and staff support. This source is clearly oriented toward the smaller library whose staff have limited experience with electronic products, and for that audience this work does a fine job.

Engeldinger, Eugene A. "Weeding of Academic Library Reference Collections: A Survey of Current Practice." *RQ* 25 (spring 1986): 366–71.

Reporting on a questionnaire sent to more than 500 U.S. colleges and universities, Engeldinger found that relatively few libraries had procedures for keeping their reference collections up-to-date. Large percentages of libraries had no written policies for reference collection development or for weeding the collection. Many indicated that without weeding, their collections would run out of shelf space in less than three years. When items were weeded, the most commonly used criteria were the age of the material and the arrival of a newer edition of a title. "Use" was considered a factor by only about half the respondents. Most libraries felt that their staff had little time to work on weeding activities. The author sums up his findings by stating that reference collections are not being managed well, in spite of the significant outlays of funds that go toward their purchase.

Evaluation of Reference and Adult Services Committee, Reference and Adult Services Division, American Library Association, ed. *The Reference Assessment Manual.* Ann Arbor, Mich.: Pierian, 1995.

A helpful essay by Anna M. Donnelly, "Reference Collection Use," provides some brief narrative about the importance of measuring such use, then offers pointers to previous studies on the subject, the need for future research, and a list of research instruments that can be used. In another essay, Ralph Lowenthal and Marjorie E. Murfin provide the same sort of research background for the use of electronic databases in reference services.

Fahey, Kathryn. "Managing a CD-ROM Collection." *MultiMedia Schools* 4 (Mar./Apr. 1997): 12–17.

Fahey presents a nuts-and-bolts approach to handling CD-ROMs in the school library. She succinctly covers the different types of CDs, networking, basic evaluation criteria, review sources, platform issues, ordering, and circulating CDs, including how to label and store them.

Ferguson, Anthony W. "Interesting Problems Encountered on My Way to Writing an Electronic Information Collection Development Statement." *Against the Grain* 7 (Apr. 1995): 16, 18–19, 90.

Summarizing his presentation from the 1994 Charleston conference, Ferguson asks four questions that seemed especially troublesome when he was writing a new collection policy: Which electronic medium best meets our user needs? Which criteria should be used for selecting titles within an access medium? Who pays for the new titles? Is the Conspectus useful for electronic collections? Many of his comments indicate that the answers are still uncertain, though the suggested options are worthy of consideration (especially for larger research libraries). One of his key points is that the requirement of creating a policy for these sources forces librarians to confront these issues and come up with at least temporary agreements on how to handle them.

Fisher, Karen. "Collection Development: Look Before You Leap for Those Who Hesitate Are Lost." In *Community College Reference Services*, edited by Bill Katz, 312–25. Metuchen, N.J.: Scarecrow, 1992.

In addition to more-general insights on collection development in the community college library, Fisher also provides a number of useful suggestions for saving funds in the reference budget. These include soliciting donated titles from local businesses and looking for special gifts for the more exciting electronic products and their hardware.

Futas, Elizabeth. "Issues in Collection Development: Ready Reference Collections." *Collection Building* 3, no. 3 (1981): 46–8.

Futas's short article gives a solid rationale for placing or removing items from the ready reference collection, something that is not present in many of the discussions of reference collection policies.

Gillespie, John T., and Ralph J. Folcarelli. *Guides to Library Collection Development.* Englewood, Colo.: Libraries Unlimited, 1994.

The bulk of this volume is an annotated bibliography of about 1,700 bibliographies and guides to the literature published between 1986 and 1993, which can be helpful to those doing collection development in those subject areas. For purposes of the present book, this volume's most useful feature is the first section, which provides an extensive, annotated list of periodicals and serials that may be used for reviews of reference materials.

Harker, Carol. "Collection Development for Electronic Materials." *Against the Grain* 7 (Apr. 1995): 21–2.

A serials vendor gives insight into some of the decisions that go into selecting electronic resources, including organizational constraints and preferences, advantages of maintaining print versions, and decisions on the best delivery methods. Harker points out that the acquisition of electronic resources will have an impact on how users access collections and what they use, in effect shaping the future direction of the collection more substantially than one might think.

Harry, Veronica, and Charles Oppenheim. "Evaluations of Electronic Databases, Part I: Criteria for Testing CDROM Products." *Online & CDROM Review* 17, no. 4 (1993): 211–22.

The authors develop a systematic framework for evaluating CD-ROM products and summarize a number of other publications that have treated the same subject. They devote more attention to the technical aspects of the products than to evaluating database content, though the assumption is that traditional reviewing does an adequate job on the latter point. A useful, detailed checklist of review items is appended to the article.

Hopkins, Richard L. "Ranking the Reference Books: Methodologies for Identifying 'Key' Reference Sources." In *Opportunities for Reference Services: The Bright Side of Reference Services in the 1990's*, edited by Bill Katz, 77–102. New York: Haworth, 1991. Also published as *The Reference Librarian*, no. 33 (1991): 77–102.

With the thousands of possible reference volumes for librarians to use in providing service, several librarians have attempted to come up with a list of the key reference sources that would be most useful in training new librarians. Hopkins reviews a number of different attempts, but finds that there was a surprising lack of consensus among these studies. He provides lists of the sources that appeared in the majority of studies, but the list is quite small. Hopkins posits that the lack of a standard short list of reference titles is due to the different personal backgrounds of those who were surveyed and the reality of different library environments and needs.

Johnson, Peggy. "Collection Development Policies and Electronic Information Sources." In *Collection Management for the 21st Century: A Handbook for Librarians*, edited by G. E. Gorman and Ruth A. Miller, 83–104. Westport, Conn.: Greenwood, 1997.

Johnson offers a strong defense for the creation of collection development policies, discussing their value in informing users and librarians, protecting the library from unreasonable outside demands, and leading to informed, consistent collection decisions. She outlines some of the additional reasons why electronic resources should be considered as a part of the collection development policy or in a separate policy, rather than being subsumed under the general rubric of "reference sources." The remainder of the chapter contains a useful review of the literature on policies for electronic resources.

———. "A Model for Improving Electronic Resources Decision-Making." *Against the Grain* 8 (Apr. 1996): 1, 16.

In a brief, informal article, Johnson describes the methods used by the University of Minnesota Libraries to select CD-ROM and on-line databases. Her outline is useful for its description of a committee designed to bring together librarians from different departments to oversee such selection. She provides background on the criteria used for choosing sources as well as the budgetary responsibilities assigned to individual librarians and the committee. The insights are applicable to small libraries as well as other research libraries.

Joswick, Kathleen E., and John P. Stierman. "Systematic Reference Weeding: A Workable Model." *Collection Management* 18, no. 1/2 (1993): 103–15.

The authors report on how they implemented a regular weeding program at Western Illinois University's main library. Using a committee made up of only reference librarians, a slow-but-steady approach to reviewing 40 to 50 titles per month was instigated at the same time a new collection development policy was crafted. Titles that at least two-thirds of the committee members recommended for removal were weeded. Results over two years demonstrated that the procedures increased the rate of weeding significantly over the sporadic attempts of the past and increased staff knowledge of the collection. The deliberate pace of the project lessened the impact on all staff involved, cataloging and circulation as well as reference, and the authors believe that the systematic approach is maintainable along with other work assignments.

Katz, William A. *Cuneiform to Computer: A History of Reference Sources*. History of the Book Series, no. 4. Lanham, Md.: Scarecrow, 1998.

Katz provides a fascinating look at the development of the various types of reference tools from ancient Babylonia through the modern age. His special concern is to portray how a reference source was produced as a result of the social and intellectual attitudes prevalent at the time of publication. The emphasis is thus more on the social aspects of reference sources than on how librarians have used them. Unfortunately, there is limited discussion of the advances in electronic sources during the last couple of decades; this is principally a well-written narrative on the reference book.

————. *Introduction to Reference Work.* 7th ed. New York: McGraw-Hill, 1997.

This two-volume textbook covers reference services and sources. The first volume offers some insights into the basics of reference librarianship, followed by an extensive treatment of reference sources arranged by type of source. Katz cites and compares a variety of reference tools in each category, and the chosen sources reveal considerable updating from his earlier editions. Electronic databases, online and CD-ROM, are incorporated into each chapter as appropriate. Katz believes that a beginning librarian should be well acquainted with between 100 and 300 key reference sources, and this text covers approximately 500 titles Katz considers basic. The book is an excellent resource for library school students and beginning librarians, as the text is both well-written and somewhat opinionated—which is valuable, coming from one of the deans of reference services writing. The strength of the work is in Katz's analysis of reference tools and the reference process. Issues such as evaluation, weeding, and collection development policies are discussed fairly briefly, however.

Kister, Kenneth F. *Kister's Best Encyclopedias: A Comparative Guide to General and Specialized Encyclopedias.* 2d ed. Phoenix: Oryx, 1994.

This is the most thorough compilation of encyclopedia reviews by the person whose name is synonymous with encyclopedia reviewing. This work contains a useful overview of the types of encyclopedias, how they are written and published, and the best ways to buy one. Kister then reviews nearly 100 general encyclopedias (dividing them into categories of "large, medium-sized, and small" encyclopedias for adults and older students and sets for children), followed by a separate chapter on electronic versions. The second part of the volume reviews more than 800 subject encyclopedias arranged under 30 subject headings. The reviews are both descriptive and evaluative; the evaluations often rank a source against its competitors. The only drawback to the work is that it becomes outdated for the more frequently revised tools.

Kluegel, Kathleen. "Revolutionary Times." *RQ* 35 (summer 1996): 453–5.

———. "The Reference Collection as Kaleidoscope." *RQ* 36 (fall 1996): 9–11.

———. "Finding Our Way." *RQ* 36 (winter 1996): 169–72.

———. "Redesigning Our Future." *RQ* 36 (spring 1997): 330–4.

A series of related columns by the then-president of the Reference and User Services Association of the American Library Association, these well-written thought pieces discuss the changes occurring in reference departments and to librarians as a result of the overwhelming movement toward electronic resources. Kluegel points out that reference collections are no longer merely the local, physical, and autonomous domain of a library's reference staff. Now collections include access to materials that are not local, and the decisions to provide these remote resources to users are often made by consortial groups rather than local reference staffs. The nature of the electronic collection changes rapidly, thus creating the "kaleidoscope" of one article's title. Just as physical spaces and signs gave users a mental map of where they needed to look for information in libraries, reference librarians need to find ways to create models for the much more amorphous electronic world. Increasing the complexity of this new era, license agreements that restrict use of resources to particular user groups but allow their use by affiliated users outside the library's walls are constricting and expanding the user population at the same time in different ways. The author suggests that one way to improve the way in which libraries cope with this new era is to redesign professional positions that combine the selection, acquisition, mediation, and interpretation of these electronic resources into the same departments and positions, thus eliminating some of the current distinctions between public and technical services.

Kroll, Rebecca. "The Place of Reference Collection Development in the Organizational Structure of the Library." *RQ* 25 (fall 1985): 96–100.

Kroll's article is one of the few that considers the staffing requirements for properly doing reference collection development. She discusses several different models of selection, pointing out the weaknesses inherent in each of them. Kroll also emphasizes the importance of providing some method of patron input for guiding the collection activities as well as for evaluating and weeding the collection after materials are acquired. Finally, she considers how the perceived nature of the reference collection as either something that indexes the local collection or that points to the broader world of information will greatly affect the sources selected for reference.

LaGuardia, Cheryl, and Stella Bentley. "Electronic Databases: Will Old Collection Development Policies Still Work?" *Online* 16 (July 1992): 60–3.

LaGuardia and Bentley's article does a succinct job of alerting librarians to the difficulties that the acquisition of electronic products causes for traditional collection development. Questions about electronic products that must be considered include: Are backfiles covered in the product? What happens to older data if there is a "roll-off" subscription? What are the search interface options? When is it better to purchase versus lease the data? What are the hardware and software requirements for the library to use the product? How much vendor support is there? What are the administrative costs? The authors contend that expectations that the usual subject selectors will be able to master the details of the new media are unrealistic. Libraries must find methods to continue using subject selectors for choosing content, but they must often include others with technical expertise to grapple with those issues. The authors conclude that current collection policies will work as a starting point as long as they are supplemented by a set of technology-based criteria that allow appropriate institutional decisions to occur.

Lea, Peter W., and Alan Day. *The Reference Sources Handbook.* London: The Library Association, 1996.

This is a basic guide to major reference tools in print at the time of publication, arranged by type of reference source. The discussion of sources is much like that of Katz's *Introduction* (q.v.), a narrative investigation of features that are important followed by descriptions of major reference titles. The work attempts to highlight the most important sources rather than to provide a comprehensive list. More attention is provided to sources in nonprint media, such as microforms, and local information and history sources than in many similar books. Published by the Library Association in London, the range of titles chosen has a pronounced British emphasis.

Luchsinger, Dale. "Developing the Reference Collection." In *Community College Reference Services,* edited by Bill Katz, 106–12. Metuchen, N.J.: Scarecrow, 1992.

Luchsinger provides a fairly basic overview of staying aware of the changing needs of the reference collection. He emphasizes the importance of working closely with faculty in judging support needed for the curriculum. A useful suggestion is that holes in the reference collection may be documented by keeping a reference desk log book in which librarians make notes about queries that were successfully and unsuccessfully answered by the current collection.

Machovec, George S. "The Retention of Print Sources in View of Electronic Databases." *Colorado Libraries* 16 (Sept. 1990): 26–8.

Although a bit dated, this article gives a succinct discussion about why libraries might cancel print subscriptions in favor of electronic versions as well as reasons why retaining the print versions might be justified. The latter issues include difficulties in using some electronic interfaces, dependable access to backfiles, use in library instruction, and ability to print or download.

Majka, David R. "An Electronic Tickler File for Reference Collection Management." *Library Software Review* 14 (fall 1995): 146–53.

Majka describes the various difficulties involved in maintaining the reference collection and proposes using "perpetual inventory management" as a basis for its control. After entering every reference title into a database program, he was able to create a system that supports regular reference weeding and manages irregular reference acquisitions as well. Details on the project's implementation are given, which reveal that the high amount of staff time needed to start the project paid off in a more well-managed collection.

———. "Reference Collection Maintenance: Theory and (Mal)Practice." *RSR: Reference Services Review* 24 (winter 1996): 67–75.

In this article Majka concisely reviews the literature on reference collection maintenance, asserting that collection development, that is, adding to the collection, is pursued more vigorously than are management activities. He considers the nature of reference collections, then proceeds to summarize writings about ongoing maintenance issues: age contrasted with use as a criterion for discarding less-useful materials, the need for continuous monitoring of the collection, the problems of irregular or pseudoserials, manual versus computer-assisted methods of maintenance, and the assignment of responsibility for conducting this work. Majka completes his review with suggestions for implementing a sound management program for the reference collection. Overall, this article does an excellent job of extracting key points from previous works on evaluating, weeding, and maintaining the collection.

Miller, Heather S. "Keeping the Lid On: Approaches to the Control of Costs in Reference Book Purchasing in an Academic Library." In *The Publishing and Review of Reference Sources,* edited by Bill Katz and Robin Kinder, 281–302. New York: Haworth, 1987. Also published as *The Reference Librarian,* no. 15 (1986): 281–302.

Noting the rapidly rising costs of reference materials in her library, Miller and her colleagues constructed a database with data on reference material prices, formats, and subjects. The database was used to review prices of all serial and standing orders. Special attention was given to items that showed unusually large increases in price. Although no information is given on the results of this project, Miller suggests several ways that libraries can save costs on reference sources, including accessing online databases while cutting subscriptions, sharing resources among different libraries, looking for lowest-price vendors, and expecting staff to stay aware of pricing developments.

Nichols, Margaret Irby. *Handbook of Reference Sources and Services for Small and Medium-Sized Libraries.* 2d ed. Austin, Texas: Texas State Library, 1994.

Aimed at public libraries in Texas that serve populations of less than 75,000 people, this source nonetheless is a valuable selection guide for all types of small libraries. Nichols lists and annotates about 900 reference sources that she has found most commonly held by these types of libraries. All of the titles were in print and available as of 1993, and order information is provided. At the end of each of the chapters, which are arranged topically, there is a list suggesting which of the serials or frequently revised sources should be updated every year, which every two years, and so on. The notes in each section occasionally cite other sources that may fill reference needs less expensively for those libraries on an especially tight budget. An additional feature of Nichols's book is a second section with brief essays on how to perform various reference activities such as conducting basic reference interviews, creating reference collection development policies, and weeding the collection.

————. *Selecting and Using a Core-Reference Collection.* 2d ed. Austin, Texas: Texas State Library, 1993.

Nichols aims this title at small, principally public libraries. In the first section she provides an annotated list of 105 reference sources that she believes are essential for any small library (or that could be the ready reference collection for a large one). Another 75 titles are described briefly in the footnotes. The author assumes that libraries using this handbook have minimal budgets, so no CD-ROM sources or expensive printed sets were included because of cost. The second section contains a well-reasoned plan for purchasing serials and updates to monographic sources on a rotating basis that minimizes any one year's budget outlay.

Norman, O. Gene. "The Impact of Electronic Information Sources on Collection Development: A Survey of Current Practice." *Library Hi Tech* 15, no. 57–58 (1997): 123–32.

Norman's useful study provides a literature review and a survey of fifteen academic libraries on changes in collection development resulting from the influx of electronic resources. His findings include changes in budgeting for materials, new methods for identifying and selecting sources, increases in the number of people involved in purchase decisions, and changes in the roles of collection development personnel. The article provides a good synthesis of earlier articles and nicely classifies the many ramifications of the rise in digital information sources.

Patrick, Gay D. *Building the Reference Collection: A How-to-Do-It Manual for School and Public Librarians.* New York: Neal-Schuman, 1992.

Oriented toward the small library, Patrick's slim volume is a practical guide for selecting materials for reference collections. A short introductory section provides some useful guidelines for setting up a reference collection development plan, including some descriptions of weeding and selecting electronic resources. The remainder of this work is principally a core bibliography of materials that will help librarians create such a plan, including sources to consult for reviews of print and electronic sources, a list of major publishers and vendors, suggestions for acquiring materials cheaply, and a replacement schedule for highly used reference tools.

Pierce, Sydney J., ed. *Weeding and Maintenance of Reference Collections.* New York: Haworth, 1990. Also published as *The Reference Librarian,* no. 29 (1990).

This was the first major collection of articles or essays dealing with the topic of weeding and reference collections. As with most of the volumes in *The Reference Librarian,* the essays range from brief, almost casual pieces to more-substantial contributions. Many of the essays report on how weeding programs were undertaken at specific libraries rather than presenting the results of research that studied a number of institutions. However, several essays are well-written, systematic considerations of issues and solutions. The many case studies are also useful, in that the situations they describe are probably quite common at U.S. libraries. Overall, this is the best single volume to read for an overview of the reference-weeding literature.

Reference Books Bulletin Editorial Board, American Library Association. *Purchasing an Encyclopedia: 12 Points to Consider.* 5th ed. Chicago: Booklist Publications, American Library Association, 1996.

A guide written for the general public, this forty-page booklet is designed to aid them in choosing adult and children's encyclopedias. The first chapter explains the major characteristics to look for in a good encyclopedia and how to go about purchasing one. Included is a nice section describing the various advantages and disadvantages of an electronic encyclopedia versus the print edition. The rest of the work provides reviews of all major sets, including updates on the 1995 editions of ten sources. The reviews are detailed but written appropriately for their intended audience. This book is useful in libraries as a guide for patrons, but reference staff should remember that reviews of newer editions appear in the ongoing *Reference Books Bulletin* insert to *Booklist.*

Reference Collection Development & Evaluation Committee, American Library Association. *Reference Collection Development: A Manual.* Chicago: American Library Association, 1991.

Building on the American Library Association's *Guide for Written Collection Development Policy Statements,* this committee paper provides an outline of the major points to consider for any reference collection development policy. The various sections are illustrated with excerpts taken from several libraries' actual policies.

Reference Collection Development & Evaluation Committee, American Library Association. "Reference Collection Development: Updated Bibliography, 1990–1997," *Reference & User Services Quarterly* 37 (winter 1997): 147–53.

This ALA committee publication contains annotations on more than fifty works dealing with reference collection development, including topics such as weeding, organization, and the selection of electronic sources. Many articles grapple with the problems caused by the increased importance of electronic products, but the compilers have excluded evaluations of specific products. The same committee published its original bibliography on this subject as *Reference Collection Development: A Bibliography,* edited by Jim Neeley, RASD Occasional Papers, no. 11 (Chicago: Reference and Adult Services Division, American Library Association, 1991).

Rettig, James. "Beyond 'Cool': Analog Models for Reviewing Digital Resources." *Online* 20 (Sept./Oct. 1996): 52–64.

———. "Bridging the Quality Gap." Paper presented as part of the "To Net or Not to Net: That Is the Question" program sponsored by the RUSA Collection Development and Evaluation Section, American Library Association Annual Conference, San Francisco, Calif., 29 June 1997. Online. Available http://swem.wm.edu/Conferences/JR/alajun97.html. 13 Apr. 1998.

Both of these papers cover similar ground, namely the problem with the quality of Internet resources for reference use. Rettig uses some delightful examples of poorly executed attempts at online reference tools, demonstrating how important it is to have reviews of these sources. Both essays also describe and evaluate the reviewing media for these resources, including Web-based, commercial sites like Yahoo and librarian-initiated tools. "Beyond 'Cool'" offers a useful comparison of the review criteria for print media with those for Web sites, essentially showing how the former work quite well to evaluate online sources without major adaptations. "Bridging the Gap" focuses on what librarians have contributed to the evaluation of Web sites so far and encourages a major cooperative effort to evaluate large portions of the Web.

Richards, Daniel T., and Dottie Eakin. *Collection Development and Assessment in Health Science Libraries.* Vol. 4 of *Current Practice in Health Sciences Librarianship,* edited by Alison Bunting. Lanham, Md.: Medical Library Association and Scarecrow Press, 1997.

A comprehensive overview of collection development issues, this title covers personnel, education, training, and budgeting issues as well as having substantial sections on evaluating print, audiovisual, software, and other electronic formats. The chapters on personnel issues in collection development are useful for many types of libraries other than just medical libraries. A short section on reference collection development considers some of the unique concerns of health sciences libraries, such as the usefulness of textbooks and multimedia formats in these reference collections.

Sader, Marion, and Amy Lewis, ed. *Encyclopedias, Atlases & Dictionaries.* New Providence, N.J.: R. R. Bowker, 1995.

This is a revision and combination of two earlier Bowker works, *Reference Books for Young Readers* and *General Reference*

Books for Adults (both published in 1988). The current title covers the indicated three major types of reference sources in print, large-print, and electronic formats. Each section begins with guidelines on what to look for in that type of reference source, followed by a number of reviews. Reviews have been written by a selected panel of experts from public, university, and a few special libraries. Each review includes "facts at a glance" and a table listing the number of pages and entries as well as the price, frequency of revision, and date reviewed. The reviews themselves are quite lengthy and detailed; most reviews—other than those for the atlases—include facsimile pages from the reviewed sources. Each provides a thorough analysis of the work's features, and a final summary gives evaluative information, some contrasts with related reference sources, and a recommendation for or against purchase. Some entries also offer citations to another review or two in the professional literature. Children's sources are considered separately from the general adult titles. Overall, this is one of the most useful and best-executed review sources. However, the length of time between editions requires users to get more-recent reviews to supplement these.

Sendi, Karen A. "Assessing the Functionality of the Reference Collection." *Collection Building* 15, no. 3 (1996): 17–21.

Sendi reports on a multifaceted study of the use of reference materials at the University of Toledo main library. Several types of usage counts were made, with the main reference collection measured via sampling during particular weeks of the year. In-house surveys were given to patrons in one portion of the study and were merely made available for interested users to complete in another; the completion rate for the first method was high, for the second, exceptionally low. A third method involved a questionnaire sent to selected instructors. The results of the study were seen as consonant with general reference staff perceptions of the collection's use. The validity of measuring collection use from only selected weeks of the year is not discussed by the author; one wonders how the timing of student assignments can affect the use patterns of individual titles. However, the ready reference collection was substantially weeded, and outdated sources in the reference stacks were weeded or replaced. Therefore, the work resulted in improved knowledge and an updating of the collection. The reported use of multiple methods to gain feedback is singular in the library literature.

Slote, Stanley J. *Weeding Library Collections: Library Weeding Methods.* 4th ed. Englewood, Colo.: Libraries Unlimited, 1997.

Slote's text is perhaps the most comprehensive publication on the subject of weeding. He has augmented his latest edition with a chapter on reference collection weeding. He describes many criteria that can be used to decide on what should be weeded, but he believes that reference sources, like those in the main collection, should be weeded if users do not remove them from the shelves after some predetermined time. Slote recommends using the spine-dotting method, in which colored dots are placed on the spine or inside the back cover of any books that reference staff reshelve. However, he notes that doing this for materials used in-house is time consuming and requires discipline to be done consistently.

Stabler, Karen Y. "Who's on First, What's on Second: Patterns of Reference Services in Academic Libraries." In *Modern Library Technology and Reference Services,* edited by Samuel T. Huang, 13–20. New York: Haworth, 1993. Also published as *The Reference Librarian,* no. 39 (1993): 13–20.

Stabler reviews the developments in library reference services over the past few decades, including the introduction of online catalogs, CD-ROMs, mediated online searching, and new electronic sources. She describes how these developments have put extra requirements (and stress) on reference librarians. Stabler contends that the latest round of changes has diminished the value of the local reference collection because remote users are increasingly finding their materials without coming into the library.

Stebelman, Scott. "The Role of Subject Specialists in Reference Collection Development," *RQ* 29 (winter 1989): 266–73.

Providing a brief overview of subject specialists in academic libraries, the article starts with the creation of these positions in

German libraries in the late nineteenth century. Stebelman then points out a number of advantages and disadvantages to using these librarians to select materials for the reference collection. Several useful suggestions for aligning subject selectors' goals with those of reference librarians are discussed.

Stevens, Norman. "Evaluating Reference Books in Theory and Practice." In *The Publishing and Review of Reference Sources*, edited by Bill Katz and Robin Kinder, 9–19. New York: Haworth, 1987. Also published as *The Reference Librarian*, no. 15 (1986): 9–19.

Stevens provides some background on his career of reviewing and selecting reference books and offers a list of the theoretical criteria that should be used to do so. However, he also points out that in practice, librarians rarely go through a list of these criteria. Instead, he argues, they look over the work for any obvious problems and features, then also consider realities such as the current state of the budget and existing sources already held by the library.

Sweetland, James H. "Reference Book Reviewing Tools: How Well Do They Do the Job?" In *The Publishing and Review of Reference Sources*, edited by Bill Katz and Robin Kinder, 65–74. New York: Haworth, 1987. Also published as *The Reference Librarian*, no. 15 (1986): 65–74.

Sweetland's study of reviews published in the major library review journals found that the reviews were too positive and often vague about whether a title should be purchased or not. Unfortunately, there was only a small degree of agreement among the journals' reviews, leading one to question their validity and usefulness.

Sylvia, Margaret, and Marcella Lesher. "Making Hard Choices: Cancelling Print Indexes." *Online* 18 (Jan. 1994): 59–64.

The coauthors believe that librarians should evaluate a number of index features before deciding to replace the print versions with CD-ROM or online versions. After providing anecdotal descriptions of several cancellations, they consider the relative merits of print versus electronic formats concerning price, ease of access, usage patterns, end results/retrieval, quality of indexing and content, and ownership. While realizing that cancellations can have other impacts on the library and that CD-ROM technology may be obsolete in the future, they believe that most students and librarians will usually prefer the electronic versions.

University of California Libraries, Collection Development Committee. *Principles for Acquiring and Licensing Information in Digital Formats.* Berkeley, Calif.: University of California Libraries, 22 May 1996. Online. Available http://sunsite.berkeley.edu/Info/principles.html. 16 May 1998.

This is meant to be an aid for University of California staff when choosing and negotiating on electronic products. Guidelines are provided for selecting resources in electronic format, considering costs, determining requirements for commercial licenses, determining the functionality expected of all products, and dealing with archival concerns.

Welch, Jeanie, Lynn A. Cauble, and Lara B. Little. "Automated Reshelving Statistics as a Tool in Reference Collection Management." *RSR: Reference Services Review* 25, no. 3–4 (1997): 79–85.

One of the preferred methods for weeding reference collections is counting the uses of materials and deselecting those that have received no or little use over a set period of time. While others had pointed to the possibilities of using bar codes and automated library systems to track these uses, until this article appeared, no one had reported an empirical study using this method. The authors gathered reshelving statistics for two years by scanning the bar codes of items removed from the shelves in reference, and then created several spreadsheets showing the use by title and by call number area. The gathered data gave those staff some hard facts on which to base their need for a major weeding of their reference collection and provided them with information that helped in the selection of new materials. Although the actual results by title and subject would not be applicable to other libraries, the methods described here should work well in most other libraries.

Wise, Suzanne. "Making Lemonade: The Challenges and Opportunities of Forced Reference Serials Cancellations; One Academic Library's Experiences." *Serials Review* 19 (winter 1993): 15–26, 96.

Wise provides details on a forced cut in her library's acquisitions budget, which required more than $30,000 in cuts from reference serials. She gives examples of how the library attempted to monitor use and get faculty feedback on the titles to cut, which was largely a successful activity. This "how-we-did-it" description is augmented with some generalizations about this sort of process and how it fits into the developing-access model of library resources as opposed to that of ownership. An eye-opening result of the cancellation project was the staff's feeling that reference services were not compromised in any significant way, which begs the question of how many unnecessary subscriptions are maintained by most libraries. Wise also includes a substantial annotated bibliography on the intersection of collection development, reference services, and serials.

Index

Christopher Nolan is head of reference and associate professor at the Elizabeth Huth Coates Library, Trinity University, San Antonio, Texas. He holds an MLS from the University of California, Los Angeles, and an MA from the School of Theology at Claremont. He has published in the areas of reference collection management, the reference interview, library instruction, government documents, and interlibrary loan. Nolan also regularly reviews reference books and Internet sources for several professional publications.